Publications by Charles R. Swindoll

ADULT BOOKS

Active Spirituality

The Bride

Compassion: Showing We Care
  in a Careless World

The Darkness and the Dawn

David: A Man of Passion
  and Destiny

Day by Day

Dear Graduate

Dropping Your Guard

Elijah: A Man of Heroism
  and Humility

Encourage Me

The Finishing Touch

Flying Closer to the Flame

For Those Who Hurt

God's Provision

The Grace Awakening

Growing Deep in the Christian Life

Growing Strong in the Seasons of Life

Growing Wise in Family Life

Hand Me Another Brick

Home: Where Life Makes Up Its Mind

Hope Again

Improving Your Serve

Intimacy with the Almighty

Joseph: A Man of Integrity
  and Forgiveness

Killing Giants, Pulling Thorns

Laugh Again

Leadership: Influence That Inspires

Living Above the Level of Mediocrity

Living Beyond the Daily Grind,
  Books I and II

The Living Insights Study Bible—
  General Editor

Living on the Ragged Edge

Make Up Your Mind

Man to Man

Moses: A Man of Selfless Dedication

The Mystery of God's Will

The Quest for Character

Recovery: When Healing Takes Time

The Road to Armageddon

Sanctity of Life

Simple Faith

Simple Trust

Starting Over

Start Where You Are

Strengthening Your Grip

Stress Fractures

Strike the Original Match

The Strong Family

Suddenly One Morning

The Tale of the Tardy Oxcart

Three Steps Forward, Two Steps Back

Victory: A Winning Game Plan for Life

Why, God?

You and Your Child

A Woman of Strength & Dignity

ESTHER

Profiles in Character from

CHARLES R. SWINDOLL

W PUBLISHING GROUP™

www.wpublishinggroup.com

A Division of Thomas Nelson, Inc.
www.ThomasNelson.com

Published by W Publishing Group, a Division of Thomas Nelson, Inc.,
P.O. Box 141000, Nashville, Tennessee 37214.

Library of Congress Cataloging-in-Publication Data

Swindoll, Charles R.
    Esther: a woman of strength & dignity: profiles in character / from Charles R.
Swindoll.
        p. cm.—(Great lives from God's word ; v. 2)
    ISBN: 0-8499-1383-7
    ISBN: 0-8499-9055-6 (Special Edition)
    1. Bible. O.T. Esther–Criticism, interpretation, etc.   2. Esther, Queen of
Persia.   3. Bible. O.T.–Biography.   I. Title.   II. Series: Swindoll, Charles R.
Great lives from God's word ; v. 2.
BS1375.2.S93   1997
222'.906–dc21   97-31487
                                                                              CIP

Printed and bound in the United States of America

04 05 06 BVG 15 14

DEDICATION

It is with great joy I
dedicate this volume to our daughter
Colleen Dane
and our daughters-in-law
Debbie Swindoll
and
Jeni Swindoll

I am confident the Lord will
graciously reward them for their
loving and faithful commitment
to their husbands
and their
deep and enduring dedication
to their children.

As He used Esther to make a difference in her times, may He use
these ladies of strength and dignity to shape and change the times
in which they live.

CONTENTS

INTRODUCTION

Esther: A Woman of Strength & Dignity

T he power of a woman!" Those words have become proverbial among us. Occasionally, they're said forcefully. Feminists are especially fond of the statement as they underscore the all-important role women play in the workplace. As the familiar bumper sticker brashly announces, "The right man for the job is *a woman.*" Sometimes that's true, even though I find myself skeptical of the put-down attitude behind it.

There are other times "the power of a woman" is said quietly, with enormous feelings of dignity and respect. Who has not watched a hurting child crawl up into the gentle arms of a mother or grandmother and seen the pain quickly dissolve? Most have witnessed a very capable woman step into a chaotic setting and bring order and meaning back into the scene. Admittedly, some women simply have the touch. Such "pioneer women" thrive on challenges—they see past the obstacles, they refuse to be intimidated by the odds. I know about these things—I married a woman like that! Most guys I know would get tired just thinking about Cynthia's to-do list. I certainly do!

Then, there's "the power of a woman" who finds herself thrust into a threatening situation that has no visible escape route. A mixture of uncertainty and danger lurks in the shadows as she finds herself virtually trapped in a no-win maze of circumstantial misery. Remarkably, she does not despair. On the contrary, she survives, she excels. It's as if she were made "for such a time as this."

Esther was that kind of woman.

Unwittingly victimized by an unbearable situation, she stepped up and determined, by God's grace, to make a difference. Throwing protocol to the wind and ignoring all her fears, this woman stood in a gap most of her peers would never have risked. In doing so, she not only exposed and foiled the plans of an evil man, who, like Adolph Hitler, had a violent agenda. She alone saved her nation from extermination. Now, that's what I call *power!*

It's that kind of stuff that makes writing this book such a delight. I mean it when I say it's got it all! When you have a story that compelling and a plot that intriguing, revolving around a woman that dynamic, you can't miss! Furthermore, you who have decided to read of her exploits will quickly discover what hidden treasures we have in this biblical character most folks have never stopped long enough to appreciate. Trust me on this one: You're going to fall in love with Esther. Then you're going to wonder how you could have lived so long without realizing what a magnificent realistic and balanced message she models, especially in this day of wild fantasies and radical extremes.

This is my second in a series of biographical studies on "Profiles in Character" from the Bible. How gratified I am with the public's overwhelmingly positive response to my first biography on David. In light of that, I couldn't wait to dig back in and write this second volume, which I've thoroughly enjoyed from start to finish. A major reason for my enjoyment of this particular project has been the "support team" of those who have worked behind the scenes to make the process run smoothly and efficiently.

Judith Markham has, again, served with great diligence and keen discernment as she has edited my original material, making helpful suggestions and giving fresh life to several sections that were gasping for air. I am also indebted to Bryce Klabunde for his attention to detail and several helpful suggestions as he checked the text for historic and linguistic accuracy. Helen Peters, my ever-efficient secretary for well over twenty years, added her magic touch on the computer and provided the footnote details that were necessary in order to complete the final draft. And then, there was David Moberg whose kind nudgings held my feet to the fire when I would have liked to ignore the deadline—*an author's dread!* His creativity with the lovely cover design helped me forget the sound of his whip. And, certainly, the patience and prayers of Cynthia, my wife of forty-two years, whose commitment knows no bounds, encourage me beyond measure. My heartfelt thanks to each one of you.

• All the way through my study of Esther, I have been reminded again and again of that twenty-fifth verse from Proverbs 31:

> Strength and dignity are her clothing,
> And she smiles at the future.

What a beautiful and certainly accurate description of Esther. The more you read, the more you will agree. But I should warn you, her story is contained in a book in the Bible that is like no other. As the late Ray Stedman describes it:

> For many this little book is a puzzle, for it seems to be out of place in the Bible. There is no mention in it of the name of God; there is no reference to worship or to faith; there is no prediction of the Messiah; there is no mention of heaven or hell—in short, there is nothing religious about it, at least on the surface. It is a gripping tale, but

might rather expect to find it in the pages of the *Reader's Digest* than the Bible.[1]

But even though her story is found in a most unusual book of the Bible, it will keep your attention from start to finish. Strange and puzzling as it may seem to the casual observer, those who look beneath the surface will find treasures they never expected.

And so, we're off on another exciting, unusual journey. The road will take several surprising twists and turns, but don't worry; we have not lost our way. We're simply following the Leader, who has a way of keeping us wondering at times where we are going and why it seems so confusing on this journey called life. But the good news is this: He knows what He is about. His way may not be as we expected, but it is the only way to go. And when you mix the power of an awesome God with the power of a godly woman, you've got a winning combination.

If you found yourself intrigued with *David: A Man of Passion and Destiny*, you're going to be enraptured with *Esther: A Woman of Strength and Dignity*.

CHUCK SWINDOLL
Dallas, Texas

A Woman of Strength & Dignity

ESTHER

CHAPTER ONE

God's Invisible Providence

G od's presence is not as intriguing as His absence. His voice is not as eloquent as His silence. Who of us has not longed for a word from God, searched for a glimpse of His power, or yearned for the reassurance of His presence, only to feel that He seems absent from the moment? Distant. Preoccupied. Maybe even unconcerned. Yet later, we realize how very present He was all along.

As far back as 1867, Walter Chalmers Smith, the Scottish preacher and poet, penned the words that have become the lyrics of one of the greatest hymns of the church:

> Immortal, invisible, God only wise,
> In light inaccessible hid from our eyes,
> Most blessed, most glorious, the Ancient of Days,
> Almighty, victorious—Thy great name we praise.
>
> Unresting, unhasting, and silent as light,
> Nor wanting, nor wasting, Thou rulest in might;
> Thy justice, like mountains, high soaring above
> Thy clouds, which are fountains of goodness and love.[2]

Though God may at times seem distant, and though He is invisible to us, He is always invincible. This is the main lesson of the Book of Esther. Though absent by name from the pages of this particular book of Jewish history, God is present in every scene and in the movement of every event, until He ultimately and finally brings everything to a marvelous climax as He proves Himself Lord of His people, the Jews.

GAINING A DEEPER UNDERSTANDING OF GOD

Before we delve into the story of Esther, I think we need to gain a deeper understanding of God so that we might grasp a greater appreciation for a book that never once names His name. To do that, let's look first at a statement Paul wrote to the Romans:

> Oh, the depth of the riches both of the wisdom and knowledge of God!
> How unsearchable are His judgments and unfathomable His ways!
>
> Romans 11:33

I can't help but believe that Paul's pen bore down hard on the parchment as he wrote those words, bringing to a climax this grand doctrinal treatise, this personal credo. Observe carefully what he says.

First, *God has a mind,* which Paul describes as "unsearchable judgments." It defies the human mind to find the depths of the mind of God—they are "unsearchable." A scholar may spend years studying another human being—his life, his writings, his work—and ultimately have a deep understanding of that person. We can plumb the depths of another's mind. But we cannot begin to scratch the surface of the unsearchable judgments of God. "My thoughts are higher than your thoughts," God told Isaiah (Isa. 55:9). Theologians have spent lifetimes searching out the traits, the characteristics, the hand of God in Scripture. Yet, those who are truly honest and humble enough to admit the truth come to the end of their earthly lives acknowledging that they have barely scratched the surface. Being God, His thoughts are beyond our ability to comprehend fully . . . His mind, beyond our ability to grasp completely.

Paul repeats words that first fell from the lips of one of Job'
and later from the prophet Isaiah:

> For who has known the mind of the LORD, or who became His

And what is the answer?
No one!
"Who has known the mind of God?"
No one!
"Who has ever given God counsel?"
No one! His mind, His judgments are unsearchabl
Furthermore, *God has a will.* But make no mistak
are "unfathomable." No human being can predict or
God's will. Try though we may, we cannot unravel the
Not fully. Not as long as we're earthbound.

Yet, wonder of wonders, God can be known d
those created in His image. As A. W. Tozer once wr

> That God can be known by the soul in tender
> while remaining infinitely aloof from the curiou
> stitutes a paradox. . . .[3]

If we come toward God with sheer reason
resisted, kept at a distance, at a loss to understan
But if we come with an open heart, in faith, we
with open arms, ready to accept, to receive, an
• When I think of the power of God, I usually
control." To me, those two words say it best.
not only of the events in Paul's day, but in the
midst of those very circumstances that today
what you're going to do, or even how you're
assured that God's power and sovereign cor
never knows frustration. He never has to scr

the world He's going to do next with people like us, or with the nations
this world.

That very power is stated clearly and beautifully in the phrases of one of
 mightiest Old Testament prophets—Daniel. He knew all about God's
earchable will and unfathomable mind. The king during the earlier years
Daniel's life was Nebuchadnezzar, a monarch who thought he was the one
overeign control of the world. That world was Babylon, a vast empire
 had taken over not only other kingdoms and strong nations, but had
 conquered the people of God, the Jews. Glorying in his great power, his
evements, and his conquests, proud Nebuchadnezzar strutted arrogantly
t his kingdom. As he walked, he reflected on himself as he said,

"Is this not Babylon the great, which I myself have built as a royal
residence by the might of my power and for the glory of my majesty?"

Daniel 4:30

en God stepped in! After informing the man "sovereignty has been
ed from you," He caused the king to lose his mind. Precisely as the
t Daniel had predicted, the king fell into a fit of insanity, to the
where he was living in the fields like a brute beast. Day after day,
ter week, year after year, dew fell on him in the mornings, rain fell
 during the day, and the cold wind wrapped its arms around him at
Nebuchadnezzar lost his reason, until God crushed him into realiz-
he was not the god of his own life—that he was not the sovereign
orld. Finally, in one glorious moment the once-proud king recog-
s, as Daniel tells us:

t at the end of that period [that is, the period of insanity] I,
uchadnezzar, raised my eyes toward heaven, and my reason returned
e, and I blessed the Most High and praised and honored Him
lives forever. . . ."

Daniel 4:34

does Nebuchadnezzar bless and praise and honor? The immortal,

4

invisible, all-wise God! The One who though invisible is invincible, and while invincible remains sovereign.

> And all the inhabitants of the earth are accounted as nothing,
> But He does according to His will [His
>   unfathomable will, guided by His unsearchable
>   mind—that's irresistible power], in the host of heaven
> And among the inhabitants of the earth;
> And no one can ward off His hand
> Or say to Him, "What hast Thou done?"
>
> Daniel 4:35

What a magnificent summation of God's sovereign control! God works among the hosts of heaven. He works in the warp and woof, in the interwoven fabric, of everyday life. He works in people like you and me, in every generation, of every year.

We live our lives under the careful, loving, gracious, albeit sovereign, hand of our God. And the movements of time and history tick off according to His reckoning, exactly as He ordained.

Back in World War II a scribble of comic graffiti began appearing on walls everywhere, proclaiming, "Kilroy was here!" This declaration was found on walls in Germany. It was found on buildings in Tokyo. It was found on big boulders in America. Kilroy was *everywhere*, it seemed.

But make no mistake, God is not like Kilroy. He does not write His name on the walls and rocks of life, but He is *there*—every day, every hour, every tick of the clock! To borrow the now-classic words of the late Francis Schaeffer, "He is there and He is not silent."[4] Never doubt the presence of God.

He is there with you on your own personal pilgrimage . . . His unsearchable mind working in concert with His unfathomable will, carrying things out under His sovereign control. I think of God's presence as "His invisible providence."

Providence. We toss the word around. But have you ever analyzed it? It comes from the Latin, *providentia. Pro* means "before" or "ahead of time";

videntia is from *videre*, meaning "to see," from which we get our word "video." [Now that should sound familiar to everyone!] Put them together, and you have "seeing ahead of time," which is what Almighty God does. He sees the events of life ahead of time—something which we of course can never do. We're great at history. Our hindsight is almost always 20/20. But we're lousy at prophecy, that is, the specifics of the future. Stop and think. We've no clue as to what will happen one minute from now, no idea what's going to happen next. But our invisible God, in his *providentia*, is continually, constantly, and confidently at work.

And you know what? Not knowing drives some of us folks crazy. It sends us into extremes of highs and lows. He blesses us, and we thank Him. He tests us, and we squirm. We weep, we grieve, we cry, we shake our heads. But in the midst of all this, He never changes. He knows what He is about, and He pursues it with relentless determination. As another stanza of Smith's hymn proclaims:

> We blossom and flourish as leaves on the tree,
> And wither and perish—but naught changeth Thee![5]

Of course not! Because He is God! He is neither fickle nor moody. He will have His way and He will not be frustrated. And if you think He has met His match with you, my friend, you are in for one back-flip surprise. If necessary, He will bring you to nothing to get your attention. He will even crush you, if need be, as He did with Nebuchadnezzar the king. Because God and God alone is calling the shots.

Now, then, you might wonder what in the world all this theology I've squeezed out of Romans 11 and Daniel 4 has to do with Esther. After all, God is not mentioned once in the Book of Esther. In fact, it is the only book in the sixty-six books of the Bible where God is not named. No prayer is offered to the name of God. No one says, "God is here!" He's not writing throughout the book, "I am God. I am in charge. I'm working these things out. I've taken charge of this woman, Esther." No. No. No. It's not like that. It's not like "Kilroy was here." He's absolutely invisible. Yet He is at work!

I love the way Matthew Henry put it:

But, though the name of God be not in it [Esther], the finger of God
is directing many minute events for the bringing about of his people's
deliverance."[6]

He doesn't sit for a pen portrait in the story of Esther, but His mind, His
will, His power, and His presence are working in concert on every page.

SEEING THE INVISIBLE WORKINGS OF GOD

In the Book of Esther, we find God's power and presence at work through
the lives of five people to carry out His will. And these five people are the
main characters of the story. We're going to see a lot of them, so it's time we
get acquainted with each one.

A King Named Ahasuerus

The first is a king whom we meet in the first two verses of the book.

> Now it took place in the days of Ahasuerus, the Ahasuerus who reigned
> from India to Ethiopia over 127 provinces, in those days as King
> Ahasuerus sat on his royal throne which was in Susa the capital, in the
> third year of his reign, he gave a banquet for all his princes and atten-
> dants, the army officers of Persia and Media, the nobles, and the princes
> of his provinces being in his presence.
>
> Esther 1:1–2

At the time Esther's story begins, Ahasuerus was only in the third year
of his twenty-one-year reign (485–465 B.C.). He was a very powerful king.
From Susa, his capital, he ruled the vast Persian empire, "from India to
Ethiopia, over 127 provinces." There was no more powerful man on earth
at that time than the Persian King Ahasuerus.

A Queen Named Vashti

The second significant person in the story is his queen, Vashti, and we
meet her only a few verses later.

Queen Vashti also gave a banquet for the women in the palace which belonged to King Ahasuerus.

Esther 1:9

Although we don't know a great deal about Queen Vashti, we do know that she was a strong-minded, independent-thinking woman who was not afraid to go against the wishes of her husband, the king. Ultimately, it is her strong-mindedness that begins the conflict in the story . . . but more about that later.

A Wicked Officer Named Haman

The third character is Haman, a wealthy and influential officer in the court of the king. In fact, he occupied the next-to-the-highest position in the kingdom, thanks to the king's promotion.

After these events King Ahasuerus promoted Haman, the son of Hammedatha the Agagite, and advanced him and established his authority over all the princes who were with him.

Esther 3:1

We'll soon get well-acquainted with Haman, the deceitful, conceited, anti-Semitic villain of the plot.

A Godly Jew Named Mordecai

The fourth person of significance in this story is a man of God named Mordecai, a Jew living in Persia.

Now there was a Jew in Susa the capital whose name was Mordecai, the son of Jair, the son of Shimei, the son of Kish, a Benjamite, who had been taken into exile from Jerusalem with the captives who had been exiled with Jeconiah king of Judah, whom Nebuchadnezzar the king of Babylon had exiled.

Esther 2:5–6

8

Many years before Esther's story begins, the Jews had a civil war, and the Jewish nation divided into the Northern and Southern Kingdoms. The Northern Kingdom was called Israel in the Scriptures. The Southern Kingdom was called Judah. Most of the kings in both kingdoms did not walk with God, at least not consistently. Eventually, God judged the people of the Northern Kingdom because of their stubborn unfaithfulness and sent the armies of Assyria against them. As a result, the Jews of the Northern Kingdom, Israel, went into bondage. More than a hundred years later, God brought similar judgment against the Jews in the Southern Kingdom because of their disobedience.

Jeconiah, was also known as Jehoiachin, the young king of Judah who reigned in 597 B.C. He wore the crown only three months when Nebuchadnezzar invaded, deported him to Babylon, and removed the temple treasures (2 Kings 24:8–17). Eleven years later, in 586 B.C., Nebuchadnezzar returned and with a vicious blow, destroyed Jerusalem and carried most of the Jews into captivity. Babylon itself fell into the hands of the Medo-Persians in 539 B.C. Ahasuerus became king of the vast Persian empire around 485 B.C., about a hundred years after the fall of Jerusalem.

The Book of Esther, then, is a slice of history from the life of the Jews living in exile in Persia. This remarkable story is proof that God did not forget them.

Mordecai was a descendant of one of those exiled Jews. He was a godly man, and his most significant role was his relationship to the fifth, and final, character of our story.

> And he was bringing up Hadassah, that is Esther, his uncle's daughter,
> for she had neither father nor mother. Now the young lady was beauti-
> ful of form and face, and when her father and her mother died,
> Mordecai took her as his own daughter.
>
> Esther 2:7

A Woman of Inner and Outer Beauty Named Esther

"Esther," which is this young woman's Persian name, means "star." This seems appropriate, since she is truly the star of the show, the heroine of the story.

The immortal, invisible, all-wise hand of God is working behind the scenes, hidden from human eyes. Only such a gracious and all-knowing Being would have His hand on some forgotten orphan, a little girl who had lost her mother and father. Only such Providence would be at work in the life of a lowly Jew living in exile in the great land of Persia, where Ahasuerus ruled in cruel sovereignty, and self-serving Haman officiated in evil deceptions.

There is a beautiful message here for anyone who has ever experienced brokenness, for anyone who has ever been crushed by life, for anyone who has ever felt that his past is so discolored, so disjointed, so fractured that there is no way in the world God can make reason and meaning out of it. We are going to learn some unforgettable lessons from Esther. Here was a little girl who must have cried her heart out at the death of her parents, bereft and orphaned, yet who years later would become key to the very survival of her people, the Jews. God and God *alone* can do such things— He, in fact, does do such things, working silently and invisibly behind the events of history.

The Plot of the Story

Let me show you just a few examples as we look at a brief overview of the plot of this great story. First, let's look at something that sounds innocuous and insignificant, but which becomes in God's unfathomable plan the link to survival.

> In those days, while Mordecai was sitting at the king's gate, Bigthan and Teresh, two of the king's officials from those who guarded the door, became angry and sought to lay hands on King Ahasuerus.
>
> Esther 2:21

Bigthan and Teresh. Even their names make them sound like a couple of thugs, don't they? Well, they are. They're the ones wearing the dark hats. "They sought to lay hands on King Ahasuerus" is just another way of saying that they were putting together an assassination game plan.

But the plot became known to Mordecai, and he told Queen Esther, and Esther informed the king in Mordecai's name.

Now when the plot was investigated and found to be so, they [Bigthan and Teresh] were both hanged on gallows; and it was written in the Book of the Chronicles in the king's presence.

Esther 2:22–23

So, what's the big deal? What does this tidbit of history have to do with anything? Who cares about Bigthan and Teresh? Nobody! Only the scribe writing down the chronicles of history. So for right now, let's put that little morsel of historical trivia on the back burner. Why? Because that seemingly insignificant fact is going to become *vital* in the plan of God. Again why? Because as we learned earlier, He is unfathomable and unsearchable, yet invincible—then as well as now.

Next, let's glance at Haman. This guy hates Mordecai not just because he's a Jew, but because Mordecai will not bow down to him. So Haman talks the king into a game plan. "If you follow my rules, I will pour money into your treasury. All I ask is that you give me the right to rid the land of all these Jews." And so King Ahasuerus, believing Haman and ignoring the brutal genocide he is plotting, passes it off with a wave of his hand, "Go ahead, do whatever you need to do."

When Mordecai gets word of what Haman is planning, he makes a crucial but dangerous decision. He must tell his adopted daughter, Esther; she must know about Haman's plan. Because, you see, by now, Esther had become queen, but nobody knew she was a Jew. When she was chosen as the king's consort, Mordecai had advised her not to tell anybody about her ethnic origins. Obediently, she didn't (Esther 2:10).

Then Mordecai told . . . Esther, "Do not imagine that you in the king's palace can escape any more than all the Jews. For if you remain silent at this time, relief and deliverance will arise for the Jews from another place and you and your father's house will perish. And who knows whether you have not attained royalty for such a time as this?"

Esther 4:13–14

Mordecai entertained no doubt that the Jews would survive this holocaust. He was convinced that God would not let His people be wiped from the face of the earth. He and Esther might be killed, but ultimately someone would deliver the Jews. However, what if God's plan was already in process? What if the means to that deliverance had already been put in place by the hand of God? What if . . . it included Esther's getting involved?

"Esther, listen!" says Mordecai. "God's hand was on my getting the message from Haman that the Jews will be killed. And God's hand was on your being appointed queen. Perhaps you were put into this position for this altogether unique hour in our history. Don't be silent. This is your greatest hour. *Speak!* Plead with the king. Stop this plot against our people!"

I've heard some people claim that they can't believe in the sovereignty of God because such a thing makes you passive. Frankly, I don't see it! Not if it stays balanced *and* biblically oriented. If anything, the sovereignty of God makes me active. It drives me before Him as I plead, "Lord, involve me in the process, if it pleases You. Activate me in Your action plan. I'm available. Speak through me. Use me."

Certainly we find no passivity in Esther. In response to Mordecai's request and admonition, she sends him this message:

> "Go, assemble all the Jews who are found in Susa, and fast for me; do not eat or drink for three days, night or day. I and my maidens also will fast in the same way. And thus I will go in to the king, which is not according to the law; and if I perish, I perish."
>
> Esther 4:16

What a courageous young woman! What training she must have received to respond like that! By the way, are you raising a daughter like that? Are you influencing her and teaching her in such a way that someday, when she faces the need for such a decision, she will say if necessary, "If I have to perish, I perish"?

I love the challenge woven into the lyrics of another grand hymn of the church:

Give of thy sons [and daughters] to bear the message glorious;
Give of thy wealth to speed them on their way;
Pour out thy soul for them in prayer victorious;
And all thou spendest Jesus will repay.[7]

▸ Do you stand beside the bedside of your little girl and boy, praying: *Lord, raise her up to be courageous, like Esther; cultivate in him the heart of a Mordecai. Speak Your message through their lips. Carry out your great plan through the life of this precious child of mine?*

The plot thickens as the excitement builds. Esther plans a banquet for the king and Haman. Blinded by his own conceit, Haman thinks the queen wants to honor him. But when the king asks Esther what request she might have that he can grant, she says, "I want both of you to come to another banquet tomorrow. Then I will tell you what I want."

Haman was thrilled! The queen was going to honor him *twice* with a feast in the presence of King Ahasuerus. *She must really think I'm something,* he thought.

On the way back home, he saw Mordecai, that Jew who would not give him the homage and deference he felt he had coming. Haman was infuriated at the sight of his nemesis. By the time he got home, however, he was once again puffed up with his own glory and recounted in detail, to his wife and all his friends, his banquet with the king and queen and his invitation for double honor the next day. Still, something stuck in his craw.

"Yet all of this does not satisfy me every time I see Mordecai the Jew sitting at the king's gate."

Esther 5:13

Meaning? "That Mordecai drives me nuts!" (Swindoll paraphrase).

Then Zeresh his wife and all his friends said to him, "Have a gallows fifty cubits high [that's seventy-five feet high] made and in the morning ask the king to have Mordecai hanged on it, then go joyfully with the king to the banquet." And the advice pleased Haman, so he had the gallows made.

Esther 5:14

But look what happens next! It's great! No, it's better than great. It's unfathomable. Unsearchable. Immortal. Look! The king can't sleep.

During that night the king could not sleep so he gave an order to bring the book of records, the chronicles, and they were read before the king.

Esther 6:1

While Haman and his gang are constructing gigantic gallows, Ahasuerus struggles with insomnia. So he orders one of his servants, "Bring the chronicles. Bring the records. Read them to me."

How ironic. The same night Haman was building gallows to hang Mordecai, Ahasuerus was listening to the history of what had happened in his kingdom during the past few years, possibly hoping the monotonous reading would put him to sleep.

And it was found written what Mordecai had reported concerning Bigthana and Teresh, two of the king's eunuchs who were doorkeepers, that they had sought to lay hands on King Ahasuerus.

Esther 6:2

When the king heard that, his mind was jerked abruptly from his desired slumber. He had overlooked Mordecai's uncovering the conspiracy against him. (Aha! Here's where that bit of "unimportant" trivia comes in!) He had forgotten that Mordecai had literally saved his neck.

And the king said, "What honor or dignity has been bestowed on Mordecai for this?" Then the king's servants who attended him said, "Nothing has been done for him."

Esther 6:3

Talk about a bizarre situation. Haman is out there building a gallows so he can kill Mordecai, and meanwhile, in the palace, in the middle of the night, the king is trying to find a way to honor Mordecai. What irony! Poetic justice at its best.

"What has been done to honor this man, Mordecai, for what he did for me?" asks Ahasuerus.

"Nothing," say his servants.

"Well, we've got to remedy that," snaps the king. "Who's in the court?"

By now, it's probably early morning, and there aren't many people stirring yet, at least not in the courtroom. But the servants check, and lo and behold, guess who's available? Haman. He's been up all night building the gallows, and he's anxious to have an audience with the king so he can further his plan to execute Mordecai. Talk about providential timing. I love it!

> So the king said, "Who is in the court?" Now Haman had just entered the outer court of the king's palace in order to speak to the king about hanging Mordecai on the gallows which he had prepared for him. And the king's servants said to him, "Behold, Haman is standing in the court." And the king said, "Let him come in." So Haman came in and the king said to him, "What is to be done for the man whom the king desires to honor?" And Haman said to himself, "Whom would the king desire to honor more than me?"
>
> Esther 6:4–6

Haman is so enamored of his own ego that he can see only himself. He's so puffed up with pride that he's about to explode. Surely the king could only be talking about him. He's the one the king wants to honor. Mentally he's rubbing his hands together, "Oh boy, oh boy, now I'm going to get what's coming to me." (Oh boy, oh boy, *is he ever!*) And he begins to list all the marvelous things that the king should do for such a person.

> Then Haman said to the king, "For the man whom the king desires to honor, let them bring a royal robe which the king has worn, and the horse on which the king has ridden, and on whose head a royal crown

has been placed; and let the robe and the horse be handed over to one of the king's most noble princes and let them array the man whom the king desires to honor and lead him on horseback through the city square, and proclaim before him, 'Thus it shall be done to the man whom the king desires to honor.'"

Esther 6:7-9

The king said, "Good idea!" (You're smiling . . . I am, too.)

Then the king said to Haman, "Take quickly the robes and the horse as you have said, and do so for Mordecai the Jew, who is sitting at the king's gate; do not fall short in anything of all that you have said."

Esther 6:10

You see, when God calls the shots, nobody can stop the action! The most powerful man in the land next to the king gets his hands tied and his mouth silenced. God and God alone can do such things.

Haman cannot believe what has just happened. He has no option but to do what the king has ordered, but when he gets home, he throws a fit.

And Haman recounted to Zeresh his wife and all his friends everything that had happened to him. Then his wise men and Zeresh his wife said to him, "If Mordecai, before whom you have begun to fall, is of Jewish origin, you will not overcome him, but will surely fall before him."

Esther 6:13

Don't you love the counsel Haman's wife unloads on him? In other words, "Don't get your hopes up, baby. You're on your way outta here" (another Swindoll paraphrase). And that's exactly what happened.

So they hanged Haman on the gallows which he prepared for Mordecai, and the king's anger subsided.

Esther 7:10

Suffering from acute depression and mental distress, verging on insanity, he turned increasingly to Christ and Christ alone for consolation. Later, he struck up a friendship with the great John Newton. Eventually, the two of them collaborated on a publication called the *Olney Hymns*, in which Newton released his best-loved hymn, "Amazing Grace." Thirteen years after his attempts at suicide, Cowper himself began writing hymns. Ultimately, he wrote sixty-seven of the hymns in that work, including this familiar one.

> God moves in a mysterious way,
> His wonders to perform;
> He plants His footsteps in the sea,
> And rides upon the storm.
>
> Deep in unfathomable mines
> Of never failing skill,
> He treasures up His bright designs,
> And works His sovereign will.
>
> Judge not the Lord by feeble sense,
> But trust Him for His grace,
> Behind a frowning providence,
> He hides a smiling face.[10]

We'll observe that "smiling face" through every twist and turn of Esther's life.

CHAPTER TWO

There She Goes—Miss Persia!

Most of our days begin rather predictably. Day after day, for the most part, we could enter into our diary the same three words: "No big deal." Days don't begin with divine skywriting. We aren't catapulted into the hours of the morning by some great recognizable movement of God, where we can sense His presence or audibly hear His voice. Angelic choirs don't awaken us with celestial harmony, blending their voices in the "Hallelujah Chorus." Normally, it's "same song, fifth verse" (or is it the sixth?).

However, days that begin uneventfully can also lead into an unbelievable, indescribable series of heart-stopping experiences. Ordinary days, in fact, can become extraordinary. They can become so different, so pivotal that they change the entire course of our life.

UNEVENTFUL BEGINNINGS—INCREDIBLE ENDINGS

Think biblically. Call a few inspiring scenes to mind. How about that morning when the rains began, resulting in the great Deluge that covered the earth and destroyed all life, save Noah and his family and the animals on the ark? Or what about that morning in the Sinai wilderness when the bush began to burn and wouldn't go out, convincing an eighty-year-old, reluctant Moses that he was to lead his people out of Egypt?

How about the morning on that Judean hillside when a Jewish teenager, tending his father's sheep as usual, heard his father, Jesse, call him inside? And before the sun set that same day, David learned he would one day be the next king of Israel!

How about the day Jesus arrived? There wasn't one citizen in Judea who awoke that morning expecting the day to bring such a life-changing event in the village of Bethlehem. Yet before that day had ended, Mary's little Lamb was born . . . and the world would never be the same.

Or, how about the morning Christ was raised from the dead? Nobody expected that—not even His closest disciples. His corpse had been placed in a grave. The grave had been sealed and was being guarded round the clock by Roman soldiers. And yet that ordinary, spring morning introduced the dawning of an incredible series of events that have affected every one of our lives.

• And finally, what about the day that hasn't happened yet—the day of Christ's return? On that glorious day, children will head off to school, loaded down with their homework and their peanut-butter-and-jelly sandwiches. Morning rush-hour traffic will choke the freeways. Merchants will be opening their doors to customers. The stock market will be abuzz with excitement and activity. Homemakers will be shopping. Planes will be taking off and landing. Judges will be sitting at their benches, hearing one case after another. Television newscasters will be busily gathering the stories of the day. Then, suddenly, in the twinkling of an eye, Christ will split the sky, and God's great plan for the future will suddenly take center stage. It could be tomorrow. *It could be today!* But whenever it is, that morning will begin as just another uneventful, ho-hum, no-big-deal kind of day.

F. B. Meyer said it so well:

> Fit yourself for God's service; be faithful. He will presently appoint
> thee. . . . In some unlikely quarter, in a shepherd's hut, or in an artisan's

cottage, God has His prepared and appointed instrument. As yet the shaft is hidden in His quiver, in the shadow of his hand; but at the precise moment at which it will tell with the greatest effect, it will be produced and launched on the air.[11]

That is exactly how it happened with Esther. She was an unknown, orphaned young woman whose life had absolutely no connection with the most powerful man in the Persian Empire. Yet God, in His providential tapestry, was weaving these two unrelated lives together. With a smiling face, He began it all on one of those ordinary kind of days. Esther's "launch" day began like any other day "in the days of Ahasuerus." In fact, her story begins as just another mundane, historical account.

JUST ANOTHER 'UNEVENTFUL' BEGINNING

Now it took place in the days of Ahasuerus, the Ahasuerus who reigned from India to Ethiopia over 127 provinces . . .

Esther 1:1

Ho-hum . . . just another king, living out another day of another year.

Before long, however, as with any story, even those that begin "Once upon a time," we notice a few unique details that make us sit up and take notice. For example, verse 3 tells us that Ahasuerus was in the third year of his reign. Put that detail on the back burner of your mind because I'll come back to it before we're through to point out the significance of it.

Then we are told that the king gave a banquet. On the surface, there's nothing unusual about that, either. Kings' banquets were common among ancient nobility, especially within that culture. This banquet, however, was an extravaganza. Observe its size and duration.

In the third year of his reign, he gave a banquet for all his princes and attendants, the army officers of Persia and Media, the nobles, and the princes of his provinces being in his presence. And he displayed the riches of his royal glory and the splendor of his great majesty for many days, 180 days.

Esther 1:3–4

Can you believe that? A 180-day banquet! We're talking six full months of banqueting, which makes today's celebrity blowouts look like stingy potlucks! For six months, every kind of exhibition and panoply displayed the majesty and glory of King Ahasuerus. Parades showed off everything from the slaves the king had made of conquered peoples to the riches he had amassed. It had all the ingredients of a pagan celebration. Loud music. Wild dancing. Too much eating. Drinking to excess. And from start to finish the praises of the king were lavishly displayed. Archaeologists excavating at Susa have unearthed inscriptions in which this king refers to himself as, "The great king. The king of kings. The king of the lands occupied by many races. The king of this great earth." Old Ahaseurus didn't struggle with an inferiority complex!

As if all this weren't enough, hard on the heels of the king's extended self-glorification, another group was invited to a second banquet.

And when these days were completed, the king gave a banquet lasting seven days for all the people who were present in Susa the capital, from the greatest to the least, in the court of the garden of the king's palace.

Esther 1:5

So this time the Persian king opens the doors and lets everybody in, from the least to the greatest. They came by the thousands, probably by the tens of thousands—for seven days.

There were hangings of fine white and violet linen held by cords of fine purple linen on silver rings and marble columns, and couches of gold and silver on a mosaic pavement of porphyry, marble, mother-of-pearl, and precious stones.

Esther 1:6

The glory of this setting must have been mind-boggling. And, as expected, there was plenty of booze.

> Drinks were served in golden vessels of various kinds, and the royal wine was plentiful according to the king's bounty.
>
> Esther 1:7

"Hold nothing back!" ordered the king. "Bring out the best wine from my own cellars. Let them have all they want."

> And the drinking was done according to the law, there was no compulsion, for so the king had given orders to each official of his household that he should do according to the desires of each person.
>
> Esther 1:8

His guests could drink a lot or a little. And if they didn't want to drink at all, that was fine, too. Each individual could do as he wished in the midst of the banqueting and revelry. This was an incredible display of majesty and power and riches. It was the celebration of a lifetime—a banquet to be remembered.

Ah, but something important was missing from the scene—the queen herself. Gini Andrews, in her richly detailed and thoroughly researched historical novel, *Esther: The Star and the Sceptre*, says that Vashti was giving her own separate banquet for the women in the palace, the wives, sisters, and mothers of the important men in Susa.

> Queen Vashti also gave a banquet for the women in the palace which belonged to King Ahasuerus.
>
> Esther 1:9

But then something happened. One of those unexpected but pivotal moments that change everything.

> On the seventh day, when the heart of the king was merry with wine, he commanded Mehuman, Biztha, Harbona, Bigtha, Abagtha, Zethar, and

Carkas, the seven eunuchs who served in the presence of King Ahasuerus, to bring Queen Vashti before the king with her royal crown in order to display her beauty to the people and the princes, for she was beautiful.

Esther 1:10–11

Inevitably, all this revelry led to excess, debauchery, and drunkenness. By now the king was drunk. And while in this inebriated state, he decided to show off another of his prizes: the physical beauty of his queen. He ordered her to be brought into the banquet hall, wearing her royal head-dress. He wanted his own private beauty pageant for all of his drunken guests to enjoy . . . and envy.

Scholars have wrestled with the meaning of the king's command. Some suggest it simply meant that Vashti was to come unveiled, which would have been scandal enough in a Persian court. Others suggest that she was to come wearing *only* her crown, which would have been another kind of scandal. But whatever it meant, the queen "just said no!"

But Queen Vashti refused to come at the king's command delivered by the eunuchs. . . .

Esther 1:12

Alexander Whyte, the nineteenth-century Scottish minister who wrote masterful character studies of both Old and New Testament characters, says of Queen Vashti:

The sacred writer makes us respect Queen Vashti amid all her disgusting surroundings. . . . whatever the royal order that came to her out of the banqueting-hall exactly was, the brave queen refused to obey it. Her beauty was her own and her husband's: it was not for open show among hundreds of half drunk men. And in the long run, the result of that night's evil work was that Vashti was dismissed into disgrace and banishment. . . . Only, let us take heed to note that the sacred writer's whole point is this, that the Divine Hand was, all the time, overruling Ahasuerus's brutality. . . .[12]

I, too, admire Queen Vashti. In the midst of an unsavory scene she was brave enough to say no to that which was blatantly wrong, and in resisting this insulting act of indignity, she took a stand against the greatest power in her universe. Good for her!

• Submission does not mean that a wife is a sexual pawn in the carnal desires of her husband. It was never God's design that a wife submit to her husband's evil desires. In King Ahasuerus's case, this took the form of desiring to display her before those who would have nothing in mind but lust. What he asked was not submission; it was sexual slavery. And I applaud Queen Vashti for her courageous decision. Marriage does not give a husband the right or the license to fulfill his basest fantasies by using his wife as a sexual object.

Having been in ministry now for more than thirty-five years, I'm virtually unshockable. But every once in a while I have to suck in my breath when I hear what some men demand of their wives, calling it submission. It is, rather, insulting and shameful. So a word of warning here: Be careful, men, what you ask of the woman God has given you. Be certain that it doesn't assault her dignity as a person, or turn a precious human being, created in God's image, into a sexual object for your own carnal gratification.

Obviously, Ahasuerus knew no such restraint, because his queen's refusal enraged him. No doubt his drunkenness contributed to this.

> The king became very angry and his wrath *burned* within him. Then the king said to the wise men who understood the times—for it was the custom of the king so to speak before all who knew law and justice, and were close to him: Carshena, Shethar, Admatha, Tarshish, Meres, Marsena, and Memucan, the seven princes of Persia and Media who had access to the king's presence and sat in the first place in the kingdom—"According to law, what is to be done with Queen Vashti, because she did not obey the command of King Ahasuerus delivered by the eunuchs?"
>
> Esther 1:12–15 (emphasis added)

Every head of state has people around who want nothing more than to please him, regardless of what this requires, and Ahasuerus was no exception.

These seven princes are named, so they cannot be confused with the seven eunuchs mentioned earlier, who were the king's household servants. These seven princes were his cabinet, his advisors, and he asked them, "What are we going to do? What's our game plan?" The queen's response had him totally baffled.

> And in the presence of the king and the princes, Memucan said, "Queen Vashti has wronged not only the king but also all the princes, and all the peoples who are in all the provinces of King Ahasuerus. For the queen's conduct will become known to all the women causing them to look with contempt on their husbands by saying, 'King Ahasuerus commanded Queen Vashti to be brought in to his presence, but she did not come.' And this day the ladies of Persia and Media who have heard of the queen's conduct will speak in the same way to all the king's princes, and there will be plenty of contempt and anger."
>
> Esther 1:16–18

I would say that's a classic example of overreaction, wouldn't you? Makes one wonder about this guy, Memucan . . . like, maybe he had trouble at home. He could use this decision as an opportunity to give his wife a message indirectly stamped with the signet of the king's ring. If so, it would help explain why he came down so hard on Vashti! He had his own self-serving agenda. Obviously, he and all the other men in the room were afraid that before long all the women in the kingdom would be doing what Queen Vashti had done. I mean, the men would lose total control of their wives!

Can't you hear this all-men's gathering, muttering and mumbling, "Yeah, that's right, man. My wife's the same way. She's already stubborn. Wait till she hears about this. There'll be no controlling her then." And on and on and on.

All of which leads Memucan to his ultimate solution:

> "If it pleases the king, let a royal edict be issued by him and let it be written in the laws of Persia and Media so that it cannot be repealed, that Vashti should come no more into the presence of King Ahasuerus,

and let the king give her royal position to another who is more worthy
than she."

Esther 1:19

So here's the outcome: Memucan wanted this edict written in to the
law of the Medes and the Persians—the law which can never be changed.
In that way, his suggestion would affect far more than Vashti; it would
have a direct effect on everyone's marriage. But if it was an attempt to get
the women of Persia to have greater respect for their husbands, it was a
strange way to make that happen!

Right about now you're probably thinking, *What in the world does all of
this have to do with righteous things? And where does Esther come in to all this?*
All we've got so far is a huge gathering at a banquet and a drunken king
and more than six months of revelry and the blatant display of carnal appetites by a bunch of insecure, frustrated men, and . . . wait a minute. Remember what we said at the beginning? God not only moves in mysterious
ways, He moves in mundane days. It may seem otherwise, but His hand is
not removed from this (or any other) scene.

If you don't believe me, just look at the final outcome of Memucan's
suggestion:

". . . and let the king give her royal position to another who is more
worthy than she."

Esther 1:19

If I may cut to the chase, four words will suffice: Exit Vashti; enter
Esther.

What you have to keep in mind is that Esther doesn't have the foggiest
idea that any of this is going on; she knows nothing of the events transpiring
in the royal palace. She also knows nothing yet about this "royal edict"
which will set events in motion that will totally change her own life. Esther
is going about her no-big-deal business, living her life, greeting the sunrise
of each ordinary morning, carrying out her day-to-day responsibilities. Is
she in for a surprise!

This is the wonder of God's sovereignty. Working behind the scenes, He is moving and pushing and rearranging events and changing minds until He brings out of even the most carnal and secular of settings a decision that will set His perfect plan in place. We see that here, and we'll see it throughout the story of Esther.

• Don't fall into the trap of thinking that God is asleep when it comes to nations, or that He is out of touch when it comes to carnal banquets, or that He sits in heaven wringing His hands when it comes to godless rulers (and foolish presidents!) who make unfair, rash, or stupid decisions. Mark it down in permanent ink: God is always at work. But His ways are so different from ours, we quickly jump to fallacious conclusions and either react rashly or get paralyzed in panic. Take a deep breath right now as you read the timeless reminder of Isaiah.

> • "For My thoughts are not your thoughts,
> Neither are your ways My ways," declares the LORD.
> "For as the heavens are higher than the earth,
> So are My ways higher than your ways,
> And My thoughts than your thoughts.
> For as the rain and the snow come down from heaven,
> And do not return there without watering the earth,
> And making it bear and sprout,
> And furnishing seed to the sower and bread to the eater;
> So shall My word be which goes forth from My mouth;
> It shall not return to Me empty,
> Without accomplishing what I desire,
> And without succeeding in the matter for which I sent it."
>
> Isaiah 55:8–11

Now, look at the rest of Memucan's ideas for the king and remember what I said about the agenda behind his radical suggestions.

> "And when the king's edict which he shall make is heard throughout all his kingdom, great as it is, then all women will give honor to their husbands, great and small."

> And this word pleased the king and the princes, and the king did as Memucan proposed. So he sent letters to all the king's provinces, to each province according to its script and to every people according to their language, that every man should be the master in his own house and the one who speaks in the language of his own people.
>
> Esther 1:20–22

Make no mistake about it, I'm all for submission, as long as it's the biblical kind of submission. And I'm certainly in favor of the husband's being the leader of the home, as long as he is God's kind of leader, set forth in Scripture, not some extreme, self-serving, and humiliating concept of leadership and submission. I'm all for the roles God has set forth for husbands and wives in His Word; I believe in them, and I declare them every chance I get. But, husbands, we don't get obedience by fiat. We don't bring about submission by legislation. And certainly not from some king whose own home and harem is in an uproar! Nevertheless, the edict goes out, and the plan begins to unfold.

Alexander Whyte completes the earlier thoughts I referred to with these applicable words:

> Let us take heed to note that the sacred writer's whole point is this, that the Divine Hand was, all the time, overruling Ahasuerus's brutality, and Vashti's brave womanliness, and Esther's beauty, and her elevation into Vashti's vacant seat, all this, and more than all this, to work together for the deliverance and the well-being of the remnant of Israel that still lay dispersed in the vast empire of Persia.[13]

Let's keep the long view in all this. In the midst of what is happening in the king's banquet hall, God's heart remains attached to His people—this remnant of Jews carried away from Zion and living in exile in Persia. To keep His promise of preservation, He must protect them from extinction, and the means to do that are at hand; the events have been set in motion to make it possible. A vacancy has opened up at the very top, in the king's household, and predictably, God has someone waiting in the wings to fill that vacancy.

Related to this, let's consider a verse in the book of Proverbs.

The king's heart is like channels of water in the hand of the LORD; He turns it wherever He wishes.

Proverbs 21:1

Doesn't that say it beautifully? Here's King Ahasuerus, who boldly proclaims himself, "The king of the world!" for six solid months. Yet all he is is a little tributary—a channel—in the hands of Almighty God.

As one contemporary lyricist puts it:

The kings of the earth and the kingdoms built by man
Rise up in their glory, then go back to dust again.[14]

God can move the hearts of the rulers of this world wherever and whenever He wishes. And, in case you've forgotten, *He is in no hurry.*

We tend to think that if God is really engaged, He will change things within the next hour or so. Certainly by sundown. Absolutely by the end of the week. But God is not a slave to the human clock. Compared to the works of mankind, He is extremely deliberate and painfully slow. As religious poet George Herbert wisely penned, "God's mill grinds slow, but sure."[15]

This is the big picture that we need to see if we are to put our anxieties on hold. God is at work. If He is able to move the hearts of kings like little channels of water "wherever He wishes," then He's able to reshape and rechannel lives that we think are unreachable, and calling their own shots, and too far gone to turn back.

The mighty "lion king" of Persia is a classic case in point. He who appeared at the beginning of the story, to be so powerful and significant, winds up drunk, is threatened by his wife's resistance, and is scrambling to stay in charge. I'm not the first to point out the humor and irony implicit in this part of the story.

Joyce Baldwin, in her small but helpful commentary of Esther, writes:

There are several ironical nuances, but the most obvious is the contrast between King Ahasuerus at the beginning of the chapter, when he is

32

the world's greatest monarch, rich and powerful, aloof yet generous, and that same king by the end of the chapter, attempting to maintain his dignity despite the defiance of his wife. This law-maker of the Persians and Medes, whose law could not be altered, was prepared to pass an edict framed in a moment of pique, when he was not even sober. The counsellors represented by Memucan were clever but hardly wise; the decree promulgated according to their advice made the king look a fool in the eyes of his subjects, and he may even have regretted the banishment of Vashti in his better moments (2:1). Is this the measure of the king who reigned over the world, and had the future of all in his power?[16]

> After these things when the anger of King Ahasuerus had subsided, he remembered Vashti and what she had done and what had been decreed against her.
>
> Esther 2:1

In setting up the next scene in the story, the writer begins, "after these things. . . ." After what things? When we read our Bible, it's important to pay attention to little particles like this, to opening lines, which we often overlook in our desire to get on with the "exciting part." In this case, however, I found that "after these things" is pregnant with meaning, including a tidbit of truth we could overlook. Remember what I told you to put on the back burner earlier: "In the third year of his reign"? Now when I read, "after these things," I thought, *Is this the fourth year of his reign or somewhere near the end of the third year of his reign?* Then I began to read through the chapter, until I came to verse 16 of chapter 2, where it says that

> Esther was taken to King Ahasuerus to his royal palace in the tenth month which is the month Tebeth, in the seventh year of his reign.
>
> Esther 2:16

Ahh! So four years have gone by in between chapters 1 and 2. But then I wondered what happened during those four years. You're wondering, too, right? So let's look at a little history. Ahasuerus (also known as Xerxes) reigned from 485 to 465 B.C. So the events of chapter 1 must have happened in 483, because that was the third year of his reign. And the events of chapter 2 must have occurred in 479, which was seven years into his reign.

History books tell us that, during that time, this particular king made an ambitious but disastrous attempt to conquer Greece. So "after these things" means that these events took place after he had led an expedition against Greece and returned home to Susa in defeat.

Picture it. . . .

Ahasuerus enters the tall, gilded palace doors, weary from battle, dispirited by defeat. He longs for someone to greet him with arms outstretched, someone who will offer words of comfort and understanding. Not just a servant or one of his officers eager to please the king, but someone who truly cares for him and his feelings. Perhaps for the first time this monarch knows true defeat and loneliness.

With all the things that have been happening, his anger against Vashti is long since forgotten. He remembers only her beauty, the warmth of her arms, and the comfort of her understanding. With his spirits at this low ebb, he goes into a period of depression. Apparently those closest to him recognize what has happened and seek to remedy it.

> Then the king's attendants, who served him, said, "Let beautiful young
> virgins be sought for the king."
>
> Esther 2:2

His servants see something happening to their master. He's moping around. He's depressed. What would cheer him up? Aha!

Now, the point is not that Ahasuerus simply needed a woman. If he was like other ancient monarchs, he had a harem full of women. Besides that, he had the power to have any woman in the kingdom. With a snap of his finger, she'd be in his presence, right there in his bedchamber. But he's not looking for a one-night encounter. He wants a wife, someone to be near him through it all, someone who would be his companion, someone who really cares, long-term.

You see, he's not drunk any longer. He's thinking clearly now. And his own needs were intensified by his loneliness.

Whether he recognized this initially, or whether it came at the suggestion of his servants, the outcome is the same. They put forth the mandate:

> "And let the king appoint overseers in all the provinces of his kingdom that they may gather every beautiful young virgin to Susa the capital, to the harem, into the custody of Hegai, the king's eunuch, who was in charge of the women; and let their cosmetics be given them. Then let the young lady who pleases the king be queen in place of Vashti." And the matter pleased the king, and he did accordingly.
>
> Esther 2:3–4

This plan would not only get a wife for the king, but would assure that she was the most beautiful woman in Persia. "We'll comb all 127 provinces, and we'll bring in every beautiful young virgin we find. We'll even let them enhance that beauty with cosmetics." In fact, notice what it says a few verses later.

> Now when the turn of each young lady came to go in to King Ahasuerus, after the end of her twelve months under the regulations for the women—for the days of their beautification were completed as follows: six months with oil of myrrh and six months with spices and the cosmetics for women . . .
>
> Esther 2:12

Look at that! It took an entire year for them to prepare these women to be presented to the king. That's a lot of Oil of Olay and Lancome, ladies and gents.

C. F. Keil, of the Keil and Delitzsch commentaries helps us understand that these words mean "to rub, to polish, signifies purification and adornment with all kind of precious ointments."[17] In other words, they spent a year preparing these women, polishing up their outward appearance, to enhance their physical beauty. Interesting, isn't it? In a relatively short period of time one's outer beauty can be enhanced, but the cultivation of beauty within—there's no short cut.

Suddenly, while the harem is cosmetic city and the king is thinking about the "Miss Persia" beauty pageant, an incredible chain of events begins to transpire, introduced by another of those little transitional phrases we could easily overlook: "Now there was a Jew in Susa."

AN UNKNOWN OLD MAN AND
AN OBSCURE YOUNG WOMAN

Let's step outside the palace and see what's happening elsewhere while God's hand prepares to move the heart of the king like a channel of water.

> Now there was a Jew in Susa the capital whose name was Mordecai, the son of Jair, the son of Shimei, the son of Kish, a Benjamite, who had been taken into exile from Jerusalem with the captives who had been exiled with Jeconiah king of Judah, whom Nebuchadnezzar the king of Babylon had exiled.
>
> Esther 2:5–6

Mordecai is totally unrelated to the king and the Persian kingdom. He's a Jew living out his years in exile. He is also raising his orphaned cousin, Hadassah.

> And he was bringing up Hadassah, that is Esther, his uncle's daughter, for she had neither father nor mother. Now the young lady was beautiful of form and face, and when her father and her mother died, Mordecai took her as his own daughter.
>
> Esther 2:7

Hadassah, her Jewish name, comes from the word for "myrtle"—a lowly shrub—and it means "fragrance." Interestingly, myrtle branches are still carried in procession at the Feast of Tabernacles, signifying peace and thanksgiving. As I mentioned earlier, her Persian name, Esther, means "star"—a reference not only to the starlike flowers of the myrtle, but like a star in the sky.

This is the first reference to Esther, and already we have learned two things about her: She was orphaned and she has grown up to become a young woman of incredible beauty. The original text is colorful, "beautiful in form and lovely to look at." Before long she will hear, "There she goes—Miss Persia," And she will win the lonely king's heart. It will be the classic example of the old proverb, "He pursued her until she captured him." But at this point, she knows nothing about palace politics or a lonely king or what the future holds for her. She is simply living out the rather uneventful days of her young life, having not the slightest inkling that she will one day be crowned the most beautiful woman in the kingdom as well as the new queen of the Persian kingdom. My, how God works!

HOW GOD STILL WORKS IN UNEVENTFUL TIMES

Woven through the tapestry of this wonderful story we find at least three timeless lessons thus far. The first has to do with God's plan. The second has to do with God's purposes. And the third has to do with God's people.

• First: *God's plans are not hindered when the events of this world are carnal or secular.* His presence penetrates, regardless, even the godless banquet halls of ancient Persia. He is not limited to working in the Christian family. He is as much at work in the Oval Office as He is in your pastor's study. He is as much at work in other countries of the world, like Iran or China or the Middle East, as He is in America. To doubt that is to draw boundaries around His sovereign control. When we do that, we can easily stop caring about our involvement in the larger events of life outside our comfort zone and familiar territory; and when that happens, we stop becoming salt and light to the world.

God is at work. He's moving. He's touching lives. He's shaping kingdoms. He's never surprised by what humanity may do. Just because actions or motives happen to be secular or carnal or unfair, it doesn't mean He's not present. Those involved may not be glorifying Him, but never doubt it, He's present. He's at work.

• Second: *God's purposes are not frustrated by moral or marital failures.* Isn't that encouraging? Especially if you have failed morally or maritally. Force yourself for the moment to imagine the debauchery of that banquet hall. The vulgarity and obscenity of the jokes. The lust in the mind of King Ahasuerus when he wanted to display his wife for the carnal pleasure of himself and his friends. The decision to divorce Vashti because she wouldn't cooperate. Yet, in spite of all that, God's purposes were not frustrated. And neither are they in your life. How do I know that? Because He is a God who applies grace to the long view of life. Wrong grieves Him and serious consequences follow, but no amount of wrong frustrates His sovereign purposes! He is a God of *great* grace.

Third: *God's people are not excluded from high places because of handicap or hardship.* I saw a sign the other day that made me smile: "Don't Even *Think* About Parking Here!" That sign came to mind when I realized my tendency to limit God's using the unusual: "Don't even *think* about discounting anybody from being in a place of significance!" God's people are not excluded from high places because they have known handicap or hardship. Esther was a Jew exiled in a foreign land. She was an orphan. She was light-years removed from Persian nobility. Yet none of that kept God from exalting her to the position where He wanted her. This makes me think of another example of such exaltation, years later, when a young couple made a long journey from their hometown, found no place to stay, and in the middle of the night caused the angels to declare, "Immanuel—God is with us." Joseph and Mary, the vehicles for the birth of the Messiah, did not come from wealth and nobility—at least not from this earth's perspective. But their son became the true King of kings and Lord of lords.

Where are you today on your own journey? Are you discounting the significance of your days? Are you sighing rather than singing? Are you wondering what good can come from all that you have to live with? The kids you can't handle? A marriage that lacks harmony? The pressures that seem to have no purpose?

God's hand is not so short that it cannot save, nor is His ear so heavy that He cannot hear. Whether you see Him or not, He is at work in your life this very moment. God specializes in turning the mundane into the meaningful. God not only moves in unusual ways, He also moves on uneventful days. He is just as involved in the mundane events as He is in the miraculous. One of my longtime friends, Howie Stevenson, often says with a smile, "God moves among the casseroles."

The stories in His Book pulsate with significance for our day and in our lives. He is a sovereign God at work amid the vast scenes of state and empires in our world. And we, even in the midst of our usual days, must remain pure and committed to the things of God and His work in our lives, even as we remain sensitive to His hand moving in carnal, secular, even drunken places. Only then can we bring to our broken world the hope it so desperately needs.

Esther does that, as we shall see, but equally important, you can do that, too. Starting today, this no-big-deal day, that seems so mundane, so commonplace, so full of, well . . . casseroles.

CHAPTER THREE

Strength and Dignity on Parade

The Bible is full of great women. So is history. Along with the Joan of Arcs and the Florence Nightingales and the Madame Curies and the Mother Teresas we find countless other nameless mothers, sisters, and daughters. Abraham Lincoln said, "No man is poor who has had a godly mother."[18] He, like many great and accomplished people, directly linked his success to his mother. Military heroes, political statesmen, ministers of the Gospel, athletes, media personalities, literary and musical geniuses alike have attributed the development and cultivation of their skills to their mothers and/or their wives. Down through the history of time marches an endless succession of courageous and visionary women, virtuous women, self-sacrificing women.

Scripture singles out some of them. This past week I participated in a little project. I thought my way through the Scriptures, from Genesis through Revelation, by calling to mind the women mentioned in God's Word. A remarkable exercise—one I recommend to you. Here are just a few who come to mind: Eve, the first wife and mother of us all; Sarah, the wife of Abraham and the mother of Isaac; Jochebed, the mother of Moses, who sacrificially kept him until he was weaned, then graciously prepared him for the court of Pharaoh where he would live for the next thirty-five years or so of his life; Hannah, the godly and devoted mother of Samuel; Abigail, the gracious and thoughtful wife of Nabal, who saved him from death by an angry David because she knew how to deal with both men. There are so many others. Deborah. Ruth. Elizabeth and Mary. Eunice and Lois. Priscilla. Lydia. Phoebe. All the way through Scripture these women keep emerging, most of them out of obscurity, only to fade again into another kind of obscurity. But each has played a major part in God's plan and has left her mark on the world.

One of those we would add, of course, is Esther, who, when we left her in the last chapter, was living in obscurity with her cousin Mordecai in the land of Persia. King Ahasuerus had returned from war, defeated, lonely, and in need of affection and long-term companionship. His counselors had advised him, "Let's find every possible available, beautiful young woman in the Persian kingdom, throughout all the provinces, and let's bring them here and let you take your pick." What they were suggesting was what we'd call today a beauty contest, plain and simple.

Josephus, the Jewish historian, tells us there were as many as 400 women involved in this rather remarkable competition. They would have a year in which to polish every seductive art, to enhance their beauty by pampering their bodies and applying the art of costume and cosmetics. Ultimately, it was intended that elegance, charm, physical beauty, and erotic seduction would carry the day. Each of them would spend a night with the king, and then he would make his choice.

Here we have the Rose Bowl queen, Miss America, and Miss Universe all rolled into one, yet with a prize bigger than any of these offer: the winner would become the queen of Persia. I rather suspect that women all over the land clamored for an opportunity to take part in this, except for one—the heroine of our story.

> Now there was a Jew in Susa the capital whose name was Mordecai. . . . And he was bringing up Hadassah, that is Esther, his uncle's daughter, for she had neither father nor mother. Now the young

lady was beautiful of form and face, and when her father and her mother died, Mordecai took her as his own daughter.

Esther 2:5a, 7

What you don't see here, but what you need to read between the lines, is that Esther was in the minority. Her people, the Jews, came to this land as captives, as the spoils of war. So she's living an obscure life, in a sheltered, monotheistic home. She was not caught up in all the hub-bub of the beauty pageant. It is obvious, however, that her physical beauty attracted someone's attention as the search got underway.

So it came about when the command and decree of the king were heard and many young ladies were gathered to Susa the capital into the custody of Hegai, that Esther was taken to the king's palace into the custody of Hegai, who was in charge of the women.

Esther 2:8

Here, I'm intrigued by the passive tense and the verb itself: "was taken." In fact, this verb can mean "taken by force," and is so rendered in other parts of the Old Testament. Some Jewish scholars give that interpretation in this passage. I don't know if there was coercion involved; we're not told that Esther was "forced" to go. But I think it would be fair to say there was reluctance on her part. Just stop and think: Why would a young Jewess want to get involved in a plan that would force her to leave the only family she had, under the guardianship of one she respected and loved, Mordecai? Why would she want to spend a year shut away in a harem, culminating in a night with a heathen king that might result in the possibility of intermarriage outside her race? No question, I think it's safe to say she went reluctantly.

Isn't it refreshing to find a little demureness in a beautiful woman? Isn't it delightful to observe true beauty, which carries with it a modesty and a disinclination to compete for honors physically? I see that in Esther and I'm impressed by it.

It doesn't take much imagination to picture the competitive spirit that must have been rife in the king's harem. Be sure of this—these women weren't spending a year cultivating great character! Can you imagine the scene? Streams of curtained litters bearing the finalists, each young woman hoping with all her heart to have her place in the sun? Imagine the petty rivalries, the in-fighting, the envy, and the jealousy. Imagine how tough it would be to maintain spiritual equilibrium when everything and everyone around you is emphasizing only the condition and shape of your body and the beauty of your face. How demeaning! How temporary and empty! Yet in the midst of all this, Esther's true beauty emerges.

> Now the young lady [Esther] pleased him [Hegai] and found favor with him. So he quickly *provided* her with her cosmetics and food, *gave* her seven choice maids from the king's palace, and *transferred* her and her maids to the best place in the harem.
>
> Esther 2:9 (emphasis added)

Remember the old song, "Whatever Lola wants, Lola gets"? Well, believe me, whatever Esther wanted, Esther could get. She not only won the favor of those who had discovered her, but also the favor of Hegai, who had powerful influence in the palace. And he says, "Whatever you want, you can have." Think of that.

But none of it goes to her head. James Hastings, whose colorful studies of biblical characters are both charming and insightful, makes this point eloquently.

> For the beauty of Esther's character is this, that she was not spoiled by her great elevation. . . . a weaker person would have been dizzy with selfish elation.
>
> . . . The orphan girl who had grown up into beauty under the care of her uncle Mordecai, . . . was lifted suddenly from sheltered obscurity into the "fierce light that beats upon a throne,"
>
> . . . The splendor of her career is seen in this very fact, that she does not succumb to the luxury of her surroundings. The royal harem among the lily-beds of Shushan is like a palace in the land of the lotus-eaters, "where it is always afternoon"; and its inmates, in their

dreamy indolence, are tempted to forget all obligations and interests beyond the obligation to please the king and their own interest in securing every comfort wealth can lavish upon them.[19]

Hastings goes on to call this harem scene "a hot-house of narcotics." This was the place to get high on seduction. This is the place where women cultivated the ability to use their charm to get what they wanted—namely, the highest office a woman could hold in the kingdom. This was the place where women had available to them all the jewelry, all the perfume, all the cosmetics, all the clothing needed to make them physically attractive and alluring to the lonely king. This was the place that would make Nordstrom's and Tiffany's, Saks Fifth Avenue, and Neiman-Marcus fade into insignificance!

Yet it is in this heady environment that Esther, God's lovely star, shines the brightest. She does this by exhibiting six queenlike traits of inner strength and godly dignity.

SIX CHARACTERISTICS OF STRENGTH AND DIGNITY

First, Esther exhibited a *grace-filled charm and elegance.*

> Now the young lady pleased him and found favor with him. So he quickly provided her with her cosmetics and food, gave her seven choice maids from the king's palace, and transferred her and her maids to the best place in the harem.
>
> Esther 2:9

In this verse, the literal translation of the original language says, "She lifted up grace before his face." Isn't that a beautiful expression? Though she was brought to the harem and participated in these things reluctantly, Esther did not display a sour attitude. I'm convinced she sensed God's hand in her situation. Why else would she have been there? Finding herself unable to say no, Esther modeled grace before the face of the king's influential servant, Hegai. What a difference between Esther and all the other women around her. Her inner qualities could not be ignored. They, in fact, captured the attention of the king's servant.

So gracious was she that Hegai quickly provided her with whatever she needed and then some. Talk about being pampered and indulged. In this place was found every emphasis imaginable on cultivating the alluring, on the sensual techniques of lovemaking, on winning the heart of a lonely king. Yet, through it all, this charming woman "lifted up grace."

* Second, Esther exhibited *an unusual restraint and control.*

> Esther did not make known her people or her kindred, for Mordecai had instructed her that she should not make them known.
>
> Esther 2:10

Esther told no one she was Jewish. Why? Because that is what Mordecai instructed her to do. Not even the head-spinning, Himalayan heights of the harem could tempt her to break her covenant with Mordecai.

God has given women an air of mystery. This is something, quite candidly, men don't have. We are a pretty predictable bunch. Yet how often I have heard a man say, "I just don't know how to figure her out. I just don't understand." For example, a woman will say, "What I need is a good cry." My friend, in all of my life I have never experienced a *good cry*. My wife knows them. Other women in our family know them. But it's a mystery to men. I'm honest, I've never been able to figure out how you can feel good after crying.

There is an air of mystery about a woman, an unpredictability that men find intriguing. Esther's ability to restrain herself only heightens the mystery—especially her verbal restraint. She knew much more than she told. She could keep a secret.

Verbal restraint is fast becoming a forgotten virtue. Thanks to tell-all tabloids and hide-nothing television talk shows, nothing is restrained. When was the last time anyone in the media blushed? Yet restraint and control always work in your favor. Learn to keep confidences, especially the confidences of your husband, your family, and your friends. Come to be known for keeping secrets! It's part of having character marked by strength and dignity.

Third, Esther sustained *a continually teachable spirit.*

> . . . Mordecai had instructed her that she should not make them
> known. . . . Esther had not yet made known her kindred or her
> people, even as Mordecai had commanded her, for Esther did what
> Mordecai told her as she had done when under his care.
>
> Esther 2:10, 20

Even becoming a finalist in this frenzied competition, or later, becoming queen, didn't cause Esther to flaunt her independence and strut her stuff. Not this lady! This lovely, dignified, wise woman was still willing to listen and learn.

She remains a sterling example for women today. Some of you are wonderfully gifted teachers. You have the ability to stand before a group and to open the Scriptures or some other area of expertise and hold an audience in rapt attention with your insight and creativity. Others of you have distinguished yourself in public service. You have played prestigious roles and offices in the community. You may be well-traveled and rather confidently move in exclusive circles with powerful men and women whom you know on a first-name basis. There is nothing wrong with any of that. But let me ask, has that changed your teachability? Do you now see yourself as the consummate authority? Or has it simply made you aware of how vast your ignorance really is? I hope it is the latter.

Someone has said, "Education is going from an unconscious to conscious awareness of one's ignorance." I agree. No one has a corner on wisdom. All the name-dropping in the world does not heighten the significance of our character. If anything, it reduces it. Our acute need is to cultivate a willingness to learn and to remain teachable. Learning from our children. Learning from friends. Learning even from our enemies. How beautiful it is to find a servant-hearted, teachable spirit among those who occupy high-profile positions of authority. Of all the qualities I look for among the men and women who comprise the student body at Dallas Theological Seminary, this is number one. Training servant-hearted leaders for the body of Christ, worldwide—that remains our top priority.

Fourth, Esther exhibited *an unselfish modesty and authenticity.*

> Now when the turn of each young lady came to go in to King
> Ahasuerus, after the end of her twelve months under the regulations
> for the women—for the days of their beautification were completed
> as follows: six months with oil of myrrh and six months with spices
> and the cosmetics for women—the young lady would go in to the
> king in this way: anything that she desired was given her to take with
> her from the harem to the king's palace. In the evening she would go
> in and in the morning she would return to the second harem, to the
> custody of Shaashgaz, the king's eunuch who was in charge of the
> concubines. She would not again go in to the king unless the king
> delighted in her and she was summoned by name.
>
> Now when the turn of Esther, the daughter of Abihail the uncle of
> Mordecai who had taken her as his daughter, came to go in to the
> king, she did not request anything except what Hegai, the king's eunuch
> who was in charge of the women, advised. And Esther found favor in
> the eyes of all who saw her.
>
> Esther 2:12-15

Think of it: no job, no responsibility, no cooking, no clean-up, no
washing, no ironing, no errands, no budget-watching, no holding back
in any area. Imagine! Pampered and indulged, in this self-centered harem
of Persia, all of the emphasis rests upon her becoming a woman of
greater physical beauty. Jewelry, clothing, perfumes, cosmetics, whatever she wishes, from coiffure to pedicure, are hers. The only thing on
everyone's mind is to win this contest—to please the king and gain his
favor.

Remember, at this time, Esther cannot be more than twenty years old or
so, and she could have been even younger. This is a chance of a lifetime for
her to have whatever she wishes. Instead, she remains true to what she has
been taught and abides by the counsel of Mordecai, believing that he knows
what is best for her. She does not succumb to the temptation around her—
the superficiality, the selfishness, the seduction, the self-centeredness. She

displays an unselfish modesty, an authenticity, amid unparalleled extravagance. I told you you'd fall in love with Esther!

> I smiled the other day when I came across the results of a survey which found that 15 percent of the women questioned tinted their hair, 22 percent wore false eyelashes, 38 percent periodically wore wigs or hairpieces, 80 percent wore rouge or some kind of facial cosmetics, 93 percent used nail polish, 98 percent wore some kind of eye makeup, and 100 percent voted in favor of a resolution condemning any kind of false packaging![20]

As ironic as that may sound, I think that most Christian women do not use cosmetics to appear false or become other than who they are. The women we admire use cosmetics to enhance the beauty that is already there. I'm sure that was true of Esther.

Frankly, I'm convinced that Esther went in to the king without fear because she had no driving ambition to be queen. Her life did not revolve around her physical appearance or making a king happy. She was there for one reason: because she knew that the hand of God was on her life, and through circumstances and Mordecai's wisdom, she had been brought to this place for a reason. To use one of my favorite expressions, she had her stuff together. She knew where she was coming from. She knew who she was. She knew what she believed. And she knew that God's hand was on her life. If it was His pleasure that she be here, if it was part of His plan, then she would willingly accept it. If not, she would willingly relinquish it. She was modest about her own person, and she was authentic.

Fifth, Esther modeled *a kind winsomeness, regardless of her surroundings.*

> . . . And Esther found favor in the eyes of all who saw her. So Esther was taken to King Ahasuerus to his royal palace in the tenth month which is the month Tebeth, in the seventh year of his reign. And the king loved Esther more than all the women, and she found favor and kindness with him more than all the virgins, so that he set the royal crown on her head and made her queen instead of Vashti.
>
> Esther 2:15, 16–17

Clearly, Esther had something about her that caused everyone to "favor" her, from the king to the women in the harem who were competing against her for his attention and affections. I think she must have had a winsomeness about her. Webster says *winsomeness* is "being pleasant, delightful, attractive in a sweet, engaging way." A person who is winsome draws you to him or to her. We are intrigued by that person's charming and gracious spirit.

Sixth, Esther displayed *a humble respect for authority.*

> Then the king gave a great banquet, Esther's banquet, for all his princes and his servants; he also made a holiday for the provinces and gave gifts according to the king's bounty.
>
> Esther had not yet made known her kindred or her people, even as Mordecai had commanded her, for Esther did what Mordecai told her as she had done when under his care.
>
> Esther 2:18, 20

Many people seem to think that when you marry you no longer need to remember parental advice. Or that when you get out on your own, you're totally and completely on your own. You think for yourself, and do whatever you want. Yet here we see that Esther, even in becoming the queen of the land, remembered the wisdom of her guardian and willingly considered his counsel.

In the past, I have shared this list of traits with my own beloved daughters, hoping that they will not only think about them but cultivate them. And it's with the same sense of care that I share these things with you today, because I personally believe they are more needed than ever in our environment of insecurity and sensuality.

PRACTICAL COUNSEL FOR MODERN-DAY ESTHERS

Now, what does all this say to the woman today? I would venture to say that all of you who have read this far in my book, in your own way, want to be a modern-day Esther. Yet such qualities seem almost unattainable. They sound so unbelievably off the chart. How can any woman even imagine having all these qualities?

It can happen. God does not mock us with the things He includes in His Word. He isn't in the business of making His people squirm under some unrealistic expectation that they can never attain—something that is totally unique to one person but remains for everyone else a frustrating and unreachable challenge. But I must quickly add, you cannot become these things by taking your cues from the world. That only brings defeat and frustration. You, as an individual, have your own pressures, your own difficulties, your own unique circumstances, but God offers ways to handle them and become His special person. The question is how? I offer two ultra-simple, but workable suggestions.

First, *ask God.* Ask him to cultivate character within you. Ask Him to give you a discontent for the superficial and a deeper desire for the spiritual. Make yourself available to His strength, His reproofs. Seek His counsel for the things you lack. Allow him to help you set reasonable goals. Record them in your journal so you will have a written account of your prayer to Him.

Anne Morrow Lindbergh, in her classic work, *Gift from the Sea*, writes this:

> I want, first of all, . . . to be at peace with myself. I want a singleness of eye, a purity of intention, a central core to my life that will enable me to carry out these obligations and activities as well as I can. I want, in fact—to borrow from the language of the saints—to live "in grace" as much of the time as possible. I am not using this term in a strictly theological sense. By grace I mean an inner harmony, essentially spiritual, which can be translated into outward harmony. I am seeking perhaps what Socrates asked for in the prayer from the Phaedrus when he said, "May the outward and inward man be one." I would like to achieve a state of inner spiritual grace from which I could function and give as I was meant to in the eye of God.[21]

Ask God to give you that kind of authenticity. To place more emphasis on what's happening deep within your heart and less emphasis on the externals, the superficial, the temporary.

* Second, *trust God*. Trust Him to control the circumstances around you—those very circumstances that you perhaps are using as an excuse for not being the woman you want to be. Don't wait for your circumstances to be perfect. (You know this: they never will be!) Remember Esther. At the height of competition, surrounded by sensual, greedy, superficial women, Esther stood alone. And, amazingly, God gave her favor in others' eyes!

Ask God. Trust God. We are completely dependent on Him for eternal life, for forgiveness, for character, for security. His light in our life gives us a growing disgust for things that merely satisfy the flesh. It shows us the importance of character, the incredible change that can come by standing alone on the things of God. He alone can give us grace and winsomeness and keep us from becoming squint-eyed, cranky Christians. It is His working in our lives that uses us even in the harems of life to make a difference and to model a charm and a beauty, a dignity and an elegance that cannot help but cause people's attention to be drawn to Him and His power.

I feel great compassion today for the woman of God who has to endure the nonsense that comes from the media regarding her role, her significance, her place in society. I don't know of anyone who has more right to be confused than the woman of today. She receives all sorts of answers, all sorts of mixed messages, all sorts of alleged proof that independence is the only way to fly and that doing your own thing and becoming what you please will bring you peace and lasting joy. Women must wonder at times, in the midst of this whirlwind, what exactly they are supposed to do. What exactly they are supposed to be.

❋ A special measure of assistance needs to be given to your daughters so they know how to be women of God in this world. Many are ready to give women a phony script.

START WHERE YOU ARE—RIGHT NOW

God has given woman a uniqueness not found in any other of His creations. It is through woman that children are born, and only through the woman. It is the mother who has the most significant influence during a child's most formative years of life. The counsel of a mother is eloquent even when not one word is spoken. Who hasn't caught "the look" from his or her mother? Who hasn't been moved to a decision by the silence of a mother, by the model of a mother, and certainly by the tears of a mother?

I believe this is true because God has given such women at least four qualities that impact our lives.

First, God has given women *a special intuition*. This is a sixth sense that allows them to penetrate the hardest shell and see beyond the thickest facade and read the truth beyond error and falsehood. Women have the ability to sense character or the lack of such, while we men seem far more gullible. Their perception is at times incredible—and on occasion maddening to us males!

Second, God has given women *an endurance to pain* that He has not given to most men, whether it is the pain of childbirth, or the ability to handle hardship over the long haul. Like the "pioneer woman" of our country's early history, they have the ability to press on against unbelievable odds with relentless determination, to persevere. I cannot number the men who have kept at the job simply because a woman in his life believed in him.

Third, along with intuition and endurance, God has given women *a unique responsiveness*. We men are far more closed—closed toward God and closed toward one another. But women have an openness, a warmth, a responsiveness to the things of God. Women have a desire to grow, to react, to feel, to show affection toward the things of God that is not found in the average man.

Fourth, God has given women *the quality of vulnerability*. Most women I know are less afraid than men to tell the truth about their lives. That's why most counselors will tell you at least 70 percent of their counselees are women. Women are willing to ask for help. If you doubt that, men, just remember the last time you were out driving and got lost, and your wife said, "Why don't we just stop and ask?" Men will drive a hundred miles out of the way just to prove that we knew where we were going. A woman will simply stop, admit she's lost, and ask for directions. Women are less guarded, less defensive. They're even willing to admit their fears and apprehensions. Women are usually the ones in the marriage who are the first to say, "There's something wrong here."

Take heart! I'm not speaking just of mothers and seasoned grandmothers. Women in general have all these qualities. If you want further proof of this, look through the Bible. God's Word is replete with examples of the strength and dignity that God has given to women. By way of example, look at several statements in Proverbs.

A gracious woman attains honor.

Proverbs 11:16a

An excellent wife is the crown of her husband.

Proverbs 12:4a

He who finds a wife finds a good thing,
And obtains favor from the LORD.

Proverbs 18:22

House and wealth are an inheritance from fathers,
But a prudent wife is from the LORD.

Proverbs 19:14

The grace of a woman brings her a place of honor. An excellent wife accords her husband a place of significance, publicly and personally. A prudent wife is a gift from God, better than any earthly inheritance. Such a woman gives her husband prudent counsel and provides her family with the leadership of reason and good sense. Her touch on her husband's arm is usually enough to slow him down or make him rethink what he's about to do or say.

The best words on woman, however, are the classic ones found in Proverbs 31:10-31. In my opinion, it is the best thing ever written about upholding the dignity and honor of women.

An excellent wife, who can find?
For her worth is far above jewels.
The heart of her husband trusts in her
And he will have no lack of gain.
She does him good and not evil
All the days of her life.

Proverbs 31:10–12

The writer then describes this woman's diligence as she carries out her role as wife and mother and businesswoman, all with efficiency, diligence, and responsibility.

And then comes my wife's favorite verse:

Strength and dignity are her clothing,
And she smiles at the future.

Proverbs 31:25

There is a strength of character and an aura of dignity about the godly woman that cannot be found even among godly men.

She opens her mouth in wisdom,
And the teaching of kindness is on her tongue.
She looks well to the ways of her household,
And does not eat the bread of idleness.
Her children rise up and bless her;
Her husband also, and he praises her, saying:
"Many daughters have done nobly,
But you excel them all."

Proverbs 31:26–29

What hope this can bring! What strength and dignity! God is so good to spell out all these qualities right about the time in this book you've begun to think that only Esther qualified. Not so! These are yours—yours for the asking, yours for the trusting. So ask! And trust!

And, lest I address all these words of this chapter to women, let me close by saying something very personal to men. My friend, my fellow-husband and fellow-dad, has God given you a woman who wishes to be like Esther, a woman of strength and dignity? If so, do you encourage her in that God-honoring pursuit? In considering your response, answer the next three questions:

1. When was the last time you told her she is God's gift to you? If it's been a while, say it again. Today.

2. How do you help her reach her long-term goals? If you're not sure what that includes, ask her to tell you. Today.

3. If you sense that she is struggling in some particular area of her life, are you there to comfort her, to reassure her? If you find that hard to do, admit it, then go ahead, and risk reaching out to her. Today.

She's worth it, you know. She just needs to know you value her as a person of strength and dignity. And, yes, she needs to know that . . . today.

Chapter Four

An Evil Interlude

Life and pain are synonymous. You cannot have one without the other. Pain is a fact of life in this fallen world, and we cannot escape it. In fact, the goal in life is not to get away from the pain of it, but to endure through it, in fact, to triumph over it, while learning the lessons only pain can teach us.

As someone put it, "Pain is inevitable. Misery is optional." Since we cannot get free of pain, the secret of successful living is finding ways to live above the level of misery. Indeed, we must.

As far back as the seventeenth century, *The New England Primer* included these words:

> Our days begin with trouble here,
> Our life is but a span,
> And cruel death is always near,
> So frail a thing is man.[22]

Even though those words were written more than three centuries ago, their sentiments find their origin in an ancient book, one of the oldest books of the Bible, the book of Job. There, in another kind of poetry, we find these words:

> Man, who is born of woman,
> Is short-lived and full of turmoil.
>
> Job 14:1

The Living Bible offers this quaint paraphrase of this verse:

> How frail is man, how few his days, how full of trouble!

How frail . . . how few . . . how full of trouble. Doesn't that say it all?

I suggest that we follow Job's example and face this reality rather than waste precious time looking for an escape from life's hardships and afflictions. In doing so, we'll learn choice lessons from these things. As old Ben Franklin used to say, "Those things that hurt, instruct."

SUFFERING: A REPEATED THEME THROUGHOUT LIFE

Stop for a moment and examine the tapestry of life. Feel the underside where all the knots and ugly thread tailings are. Observe the suffering that is woven through the fabric of humanity.

Feel, for example, the natural world where every year we live through "natural disasters" such as tornadoes, floods, volcanoes, earthquakes, tidal waves, monsoons, droughts, hurricanes, mud slides, ice storms, dust storms, hail storms, and blizzards.

In the physical world, babies are born with severe birth defects, with heartbreaking disabilities and handicaps. Horrible accidents lead to debilitating injuries, to life-threatening and scarring burns. People by the millions live with chronic pain. Diseases bring indignities, suffering, isolation, and often death.

In the emotional world, many face the horrors of recurring depression, discouragement, and disappointment. Neuroses and psychoses and a host of related problems plague people's lives.

Then there is the domestic world, where the news is filled with the stories of battered spouses and abused, not to mention neglected or abandoned, children—scenes so horrible that they are beyond imagining. One statistic reports that every fifteen seconds there are those kind of domestic conflicts. Another report, from one of our nation's respected universities several years ago, stated that the only place more dangerous to live than amid riots and war is the American home."

On the national and international scene there are "troubled spots," "hot spots," conflicts and skirmishes, some that have escalated into world wars.

I could spend pages giving you examples that life and pain are synonymous. You can't get away from it.

The best way to begin living with and learning from such experiences is to understand the theological root of the problem. It is the universal presence of evil, plain and simple. The inescapable reality of sin. I believe that Adam and Eve would have lived forever, free of disease and every other form of pain, had they not sinned. But with the coming of sin came the curse of pain and suffering, ultimately, the sorrow of death. Evil is always there, lurking in the shadows, quick to invade and violate.

This is true, even though right now, today, you may feel that your life is in pretty good shape. You're healthy and economically comfortable. You're aging but you're not sick. You have good family relationships. You may be tempted at this time of your life to sit back on your haunches and think, I can make it through the rest of my days. If so, all I can say is, *Don't count on it*. You are not living on Cloud Nine. You're just like the rest of us, riveted to planet earth. Ours is an evil society, and it's not only because the other guy is wrong; it's because *you and I are wrong*. Sin is a universal disease. As a result, we live in its backwash. It fractures partnerships. It ruins marriages. It splits churches. It prompts wicked thoughts and plans. It dissolves friendships. It paralyzes goals. It shatters dreams.

Even in the lovely, Cinderella story of Esther evil rears its ugly head, just when everything's about to turn out right. King Ahasuerus has found a wife, a young woman who is beautiful inside and out. The lovely, modest orphan girl has been crowned queen. Ahasuerus is delighted. Mordecai's pleased. Esther's surprised and no doubt very grateful. The nation rejoices.

But then comes an evil interlude that disrupts everything beautiful. Why should we be amazed? It happens in life, time after time after time. Not even in biblical days did people "live happily ever after."

MUTINY: A MINOR PLOT AGAINST THE KING

As is often true with evil, it surfaced ever so quietly. While the majority in the kingdom were pleased with the way things were going, a secret conspiracy was growing in the minds of two men.

> In those days, while Mordecai was sitting at the king's gate, Bigthan and Teresh, two of the king's officials from those who guarded the door, became angry and sought to lay hands on King Ahasuerus.
>
> Esther 2:21

"In those days." In *what* days? In days when the king and the people were banqueting and rejoicing, when everybody seemed so satisfied and pleased and at peace with one another.

Isn't that the way it is? I mean, why couldn't these two guards have just forgiven the king? Why couldn't they have shrugged off the fact that he did something or said something that ticked them off? Why couldn't Bigthan have said to Teresh, "Hey, don't let it bother you. The guy's got a lot on his mind." Whatever it was, it wasn't worth a conspiracy. And it certainly wasn't worth a planned assassination. But that's the way evil is. When an offense isn't checked, it grows into anger. And when anger is allowed to fester, it leads to rage and sometimes to murder. When those kinds of things poison our minds, they can make us into people bent on conspiracy.

Such is the case with these two men, and before long their anger leads to a murderous plan.

> But the plot became known to Mordecai, and he told Queen Esther, and Esther informed the king in Mordecai's name. Now when the plot was investigated and found to be so, they were both hanged on a

gallows; and it was written in the Book of Chronicles in the king's presence.

Esther 2:22–23

In those days, under the regime of Persian rule, they didn't mess around with a lot of time in a courtroom. If a king's life was endangered, those responsible paid for it with their lives. Swiftly. So . . . that's the end of Bigthan and Teresh and their plot, but it is not the end of evil, or the consequences of what they have done. Just remember this incident. We'll encounter it again in Esther's life.

Because they yielded to their evil imaginations, these two men got themselves involved in a plot that finally resulted in their own deaths. However, lest we study this section of Scripture and what follows thinking how wicked people were in the days of Persia, I want us to remember that latent within every heart are thoughts of rage and murder, as well as greed and lust and abuse—the seamy, ugly side of life. You and I have it deep within our hearts. And were it not for the power of the living God, acts of violence would be committed by every one of us, and we would finally exterminate ourselves off the face of this planet.

Those two bodies impaled on the gallows were a reminder for all the people of Persia: This is evil. This is the result of evil. The scene was horrible, made no mistake about it.

> Rather than being hanged by the neck on a modern-type gallows, the men were probably impaled on a stake or post (cf. Ezra 6:11). This was not an unusual method of execution in the Persian Empire. Darius, Xerxes' father, was known to have once impaled 3,000 men. A record of this assassination attempt was written in **the annals**, the official royal record (cf. Es. 6:1–2).[23]

In ancient days, they stopped at nothing to create fear in the hearts of every citizen so all would know that crime does not pay. But even with a ghastly scene as horrible as two men impaled on public gallows, evil did not go away.

VENGEANCE: A MAJOR SCHEME AGAINST THE JEWS

"After these events" (3:1) an even greater evil enters the scene. Isn't it interesting how these sections tie together with these rather innocuous phrases: "after these things," "so it came about," "in those days," "after these events"? That's the way it is in life. The big events in our lives, the major turning points, don't begin with a bold, ear-splitting announcement from heaven, "Today will bring trouble—*bad* trouble!" No, those days begin like every other morning. You have no idea it's coming. And out of the blue it strikes! And you find yourself in the midst of this ancient struggle with sin and evil.

> After these events King Ahasuerus promoted Haman, the son of Hammedatha the Agagite, and advanced him and established his authority over all the princes who were with him.
>
> Esther 3:1

Now, wait a minute! What's going on here? Mordecai's the one who saved the king's life. Right? Mordecai's the one who told Esther, who then told the king. Mordecai's the one who uncovered the plot and saved the king's life. So why is Haman getting the promotion?

I forgot to tell you: Life's not only painful; it's also unfair. Perhaps you are thinking right now that you will be promoted because *you* have worked the hardest, *you* have come up with the big ideas, *you* are the one who's done the most for your boss; therefore, it's only right that *you* be given that special position you've been anticipating. Well, be prepared. It probably won't happen. I'm not trying to be pessimistic, just realistic. Wrong happens! Because life isn't fair. Why? Because of evil.

When righteousness rules, justice reigns; but when evil lurks in a heart, injustice follows. And that's exactly what happens when Haman, of all people, is advanced, given authority, and promoted.

> And all the kings servants who were at the king's gate bowed down and paid homage to Haman; for so the king had commanded concerning him. But Mordecai neither bowed down nor paid homage.
>
> Esther 3:2

You say, "Aha! This guy had a bad attitude." No, Mordecai was a Jew. And to a Jew, bowing down to any person or thing on this earth was considered idolatry. It went against the deepest convictions of his faith. The Torah states clearly: "You shall have no other gods before Me." So Mordecai would not bow down and pay homage to anyone.

When he is asked about why he will not obey the king's command— why he will not pay homage to the man the king has promoted to a place of authority—Mordecai has his answer ready.

> Then the king's servants who were at the king's gate said to Mordecai, "Why are you transgressing the king's command?"
>
> Now it was when they had spoken daily to him and he would not listen to them, that they told Haman to see whether Mordecai's reason would stand; for he had told them that he was a Jew.
>
> Esther 3:3–4

Obviously, the king's servants hounded Mordecai about this for several days. And each time they raised the issue he told them the same thing: "I am a Jew" (which being interpreted, meant, "I cannot bow down to any earthly being.") And the troublemaking evil in their hearts leads them to report this to Haman.

> When Haman saw that Mordecai neither bowed down nor paid homage to him, Haman was filled with *rage*. But he disdained to lay hands on Mordecai alone, for they had told him who the people of Mordecai were; therefore Haman sought *to destroy all the Jews*, the people of Mordecai, who were throughout the whole kingdom of Ahasuerus.
>
> Esther 3:5–6 (emphasis added)

What's happening here? Why would Mordecai's refusal to bow down to Haman cause Haman to become enraged and then want to kill all the Jews? Even wanting to retaliate and kill Mordecai would be excessively evil, but to kill an entire people, who are in no way involved in this private battle of wills?

The answer is that all this goes back to an old grudge. Take another look at that bit of genealogy mentioned in verse 1: "Ahasuerus promoted Haman, the son of Hammedatha the *Agagite*."

If you know your biblical history, you know that tucked away in the folds of 1 Samuel is an interesting story about a king named Saul who was told by a prophet named Samuel to kill the Amalekites, the lifelong enemy of the Jews. The Amalekites had attacked Israel after they left Egypt; that's how far back this adversarial relationship went. So Saul was instructed to kill all the Amalekites, along with all their animals. But Saul, pragmatist that he was, saved the best of the enemy's sheep. He also spared the king, Agag. And the Agagites, descendants of the Amalekites, got their name from the king that Saul didn't kill. (Which should be an excellent reminder that when God tells you to do something, you'd better do it; He always has a reason.) Afterward, the prophet Samuel confronted Saul about his disobedience. And after Saul danced around with some verbal semantic footwork while rationalizing his disobedience, he finally confessed that he had failed to do as the Lord had commanded. Then Samuel "put Agag to death before the Lord" (1 Sam. 15:33).

For all these years since, these age-old enemies of the Jews had passed this scene from their history down through succeeding generations. As a result, the Agagites *hated the Jews!* And Haman being an Agagite, had been nursing a grudge which had been taught him since childhood.

This is a good time to mention that no one is born with grudges. Prejudice is not a package deal that comes with birth. It's something we learn; we're trained in it. We're not born hating. We must be taught to hate.

I have a friend who once lived in a state in the Deep South who found himself shocked that the Ku Klux Klan still held marches down the main street of their city. In those marches were children, as well as their parents, wearing white hoods. Those kids are being trained to hate as their fathers hate.

From his parents and grandparents and great-grandparents, from his uncles and aunts and cousins, Haman the Agagite had learned to hate the Jews. That hatred ate away at him, and when he was placed in a position of power, we can be certain he carried that hatred with him. He wore it like a mantle.

In my Bible I have circled the words: "Haman sought to destroy all the

Jews." Because, you see, that's the way evil is. It grows in an exaggerated manner. Thus, Haman's not satisfied simply to kill Mordecai or to make his life miserable. He's now on a self-appointed mission, not unlike Adolph Hitler in the 1930s and 1940s, to kill all of Mordecai's people.

His anti-Semitic extermination plan unfolds quickly and imaginatively, spurred on by evil. It also gets ugly.

> In the first month, which is the month Nisan, in the twelfth year of King Ahasuerus, Pur, that is the lot, was cast before Haman from day to day and from month to month, until the twelfth month, that is the month Adar.
>
> Esther 3:7

In *The Queen and I*, Ray Stedman's fine little book on Esther, he provides helpful clarification of this casting of lots:

What a strange procedure! But the casting of lots to determine a lucky day on which to do something was common practice in oriental king-doms. It is very similar to the practice today of shooting dice in order to select a propitious day for some activity. When the record says, "They cast it month after month till the twelfth month," it doesn't mean they shook dice for a whole year in front of Haman. It means that every cast made stood for a different day. A cast was made for each day of the calendar and if a propitious number [we might say, an evil omen, or some sense of significance aroused by the throwing of the dice] turned up that day was regarded as a lucky day; thus they went through 365 casts before they found the lucky day. When they found it, it was in the twelfth month called the month of Adar. This whole process made it possible for Haman to go to the king and say, "Look! If you really want good luck in your life, if you want fortune to smile upon you, there's only one thing to do—get rid of these people!"[24]

When your life is driven by superstition, you come up with some ridiculous ideas and decisions. Stupid things. Sometimes, *demonic things!*

Which is exactly what happened here.

> Then Haman said to King Ahasuerus, "There is a certain people scattered and dispersed among the peoples in all the provinces of your kingdom; their laws are different from those of all other people, and they do not observe the king's laws, so it is not in the king's interest to let them remain."
>
> Esther 3:8

We are witnessing an escalation of evil before our eyes. What began as anger turned to prejudice. Hatred has grown now to murder in Haman's mind. This is nothing more than extermination talk. Haman is telling the king what the king wants to hear, but he's not telling the king the whole story. Haman doesn't mention his own prejudice, his own long-standing prejudiced grudge—the ugly anti-Semitism that goes back to his Amalekite roots. No, he deliberately hides his real motive while acting as if he has only the king's good at heart.

The king has no one to advise him wisely. No one with the objectivity to stand back and say, "Whoa! There's a lot more to this than meets the eye. This guy is prejudiced. He's not concerned about your good, or the good of the kingdom. He's pushing his own agenda here." When you have a prejudiced counselor, and he or she is the only person giving you information, you ultimately come up with destructive plans or decisions. This is why it is important that each of us lives an accountable life and includes in our circle people who are strong enough to use words like: "unwise," "not good," "too far," "watch it."

King Ahasuerus apparently had none of that, so when Haman came up with his extermination plan for the Jews, the king fell for it, hook, line, and sinker. He loved the idea. It appealed to his superstition, his conceit and his greed. Haman knew which buttons to push.

> "If it is pleasing to the king, let it be decreed that they be destroyed, and I will pay ten thousand talents of silver into the hands of those who carry on the king's business, to put into the king's treasuries."
>
> Esther 3:9

Ten thousand talents of silver. That was 375 tons of silver! In that day Persia used silver as its monetary standard, so that represented a lot of loot. Where would Haman get it? Probably from the homes and possessions he would confiscate once he killed the Jews.

> Then the king took his signet ring from his hand and gave it to Haman,
> the son of Hammedatha the Agagite, the enemy of the Jews.
>
> Esther 3:10

Which is like giving your MasterCard to your associate and saying, "Ring it up!"

The king's signet ring contained an inscription that was the unique official seal. With it, he signed decrees and other documents by impressing the seal on clay, giving them his sanction. For example, an edict would be written on a scroll; the scroll would be rolled up and sealed shut with a small wad of soft clay; then the king would press his signet ring into the clay, leaving the impression of the inscription. This meant, "Let it be written" or "Let it be done." That was the significance of the ring he gave to Haman. In acquiescing, the king literally stamped his official approval on this hideous plan—a plan that would include the Jewish queen, Esther herself, though at the time he had no knowledge of that. When an evil plan gets underway, there are *always* unknown areas of wickedness no one thinks about ahead of time.

> And the king said to Haman, "The silver is yours, and the people also,
> to do with them as you please."
>
> Esther 3:11

Again, there are overtones here that sound a lot like Hitler in the 1930s, aren't there? What has happened to Ahasuerus that he can say, with the wave of his hand, "Just finish them off"? It's almost more than our minds can imagine.

However, before we turn our thoughts to Hitler or other evil madmen of the ages, let's get painfully honest and look a little closer to home. Are you nursing a grudge? Do you have someone's face on your dart board? To help prompt an honest answer, may I make some suggestions? Folks like a former spouse, former pastor, a former roommate, a church that offended you, an organization that took unfair advantage of you, a boss, a coach, someone you revered and trusted who used you and/or abused you? Do you have someone who has made life difficult for you and has never "made it right"? And although they are now out of your life—physically absent—the incident in the past is still vivid in your memory, deepening your determination to hold onto them. If such is true, unless I miss my guess here, you entertain thoughts like, "*Someday, some way* I'll get back!" This nursing of anger, this lingering grudge, this deliberate refusal to forgive festers and grows. It's silent. Oh, it's so silent. And so deadly!

Haman is an adult by the time we meet him. We don't know how old he is, but given his position, he's no teenager. And he comes into this official position ready to pounce. This is his *moment,* and he's going to take it!

Life and pain are synonymous. We cannot escape the pain. And if we're not careful, that pain can cause us to carry out the most heinous of sins.

Our courts are filled with terrible criminal cases. Stalkers, slashers, terrorists, abusers, murderers, even serial killers. We read of a man who has killed sixty people—murdered them in the most gruesome of ways. We watch him sit in court and smile through his trial, and we think, *What an animal!* And so he may be. But what is easy to ignore is this: The same animal-like nature resides in me, and it resides in you. It is wicked to the core. It is vile beyond belief. And were it not for the presence of grace and the miraculous deliverance of Jesus Christ at work within us, controlling our passions and urging us to forgive and move on, it would *consume us.* And we would *kill* and not give it a second thought.

How absolutely powerless we are to solve our own inner problem of evil. Were not the power of the Holy Spirit given to me in daily doses, literally moment-by-moment doses, my grudges, my lack of forgiveness could grow into thoughts that would shock you. And yours would shock me.

That's what happened to Haman. That's why he could devise his wicked plan. That's why he could commit this evil without a second thought. He had no inner power from the living God to stop him, to help him get rid of his hatred and prejudice, to live above revenge's powerful grip.

And as a result? He pressed on without hesitation, without a hint of restraint or glimmer of guilt.

> Then the king's scribes were summoned on the thirteenth day of the first month, and it was written just as Haman commanded to the king's satraps, to the governors who were over each province, and to the princes of each people, each province according to its script, each people according to its language, being written in the name of King Ahasuerus and sealed with the king's signet ring. And letters were sent by couriers to all the king's provinces to destroy, to kill, and to annihilate all the Jews, both young and old, women and children, in one day, the thirteenth day of the twelfth month, which is the month Adar, and to seize their possessions as plunder.
>
> Esther 3:12–13

Did you track the scene? Haman ordered the annihilation of all the Jews throughout each of the 127 provinces of the kingdom. He had the extermination plan put into writing, and he sealed it with the king's ring, in the first month of the year, but it was not to be carried out until the twelfth month. *Let them live in the misery, knowing what awaits them,* he must have thought. He not only wanted to kill them; he wanted to torture them.

> A copy of the edict to be issued as law in every province was published to all the people so that they should be ready for this day.
>
> The couriers went out impelled by the king's command while the decree was issued in Susa the capital; and while the king and Haman sat down to drink, the city of Susa was in confusion.
>
> Esther 3:14–15

Yes, such murderous things can be planned. And all the while you can sip your booze and care less as others around you live in misery. That's the way it is with unchecked evil.

WICKEDNESS: AN APPROPRIATE RESPONSE

Though we are far from finished with this remarkably relevant story, it's time we paused and caught our breath. Already, we can draw <u>three very valuable lessons</u> from three major characters of this story. First from Mordecai, and then from Haman, and finally from Ahasuerus.

First, from Mordecai we learn: *Never forget there will always be someone who will resent your devotion to the Lord.*

That's how it all started in Persia, remember?

"Why don't you bow down to Haman the prime minister?"

"I am a Jew. My devotion to my Lord is such that I dare not do that." The result was a resentment so severe it triggered an extermination plot!

There will always be someone who will resent your devotion to the Lord. Expect it. If you don't, you will allow your will to be weakened. I've seen it in the military. I've seen it in neighborhoods. I've seen it in ministry. I've certainly seen it in the business world, where pressure intensifies because a person's convictions cut across "company policy." The results get so ugly, I've known some who simply could not remain a part of the firm.

Second, from Haman we learn: *Never underestimate the diabolical nature of revenge.* And while I'm at it, don't underestimate your own ability to connive and retaliate. A lack of forgiveness that stays on the back burner has the ability to poison your life if you allow it. Many a divorced person today is consumed by the poison of an unforgiving spirit. How many young-to-middle-aged adults have turned on their parents rather than forgiven them? How many vicious acts of terrorism have been spawned in polluted streams of unforgiveness?

Third, from Ahasuerus: *Never overestimate the value of your own importance.* It's so easy to be blinded by one's own pride of position and power. Some wise counselor should have had access to King Ahasuerus and been allowed to say to him, "What is this terrible thing that you're permitting? It isn't worth it. Not even you are that important."

In every life, "an evil interlude" is never very far away—a secret plan to walk away from God-given responsibilities or a smoldering spirit that, if not dealt with, can lead to violence, even murder.

As I write these words, the final decision of a federal jury in Denver, Colorado, has just been announced. A man has not only been found guilty of murder, but condemned to death for the April 19, 1995, bombing of a federal office building in Oklahoma City. Tragically, that bombing killed 168 men, women, and children and injured hundreds more. Only twenty-nine years old, the Persian Gulf War veteran committed this heinous act of random political terror, because he allowed a spirit of unforgiveness and bitterness to grow into blind rage, which ultimately led him to commit the most dreadful act of mass murder by an American in American history. His own "evil interlude" fed by the poison of hateful prejudice, has imprinted on our minds a name that will go down in infamy—a name we'll never forget: Timothy McVeigh.

To this day the Jews have never forgotten the man named Haman. They're reminded of him each year at the Feast of Purim.

> During the dramatic reading of the Book of Esther in a Jewish synagogue at the Feast of Purim, the congregation may be found taking the part of a chorus and exclaiming at every mention of the name of Haman, "May his name be blotted out," "Let the name of the ungodly perish," while boys with mallets will pound stones and bits of wood on which the odious name is written.[25]

At one time or another in every one of our lives we have been *shocked* with the relevance of Scripture. It has cut like a hot knife through butter deep into our hearts. That should certainly hold true regarding the effect of evil we see in Haman's life. But the truth is, it holds true in our own lives as well. If we allow our anger and our grudges to fester, if we make plans for revenge, we will quite likely end up doing horrible things to others and ourselves.

It is for this very reason that God invaded our polluted world in the Person of His Son, Jesus Christ. We're not able to help ourselves, but the Lord Jesus can. He opened the door to forgiveness and power on the cross on which He was placed. He let nails be driven into His hands and feet, and He hung and died there, so that whoever would believe in Him would never perish in their own sin and evil. Somehow, in some wonderful way, the blood that came from His body serves as an internal detergent that washes away our sins. No words I could give you, or that anyone could give you, will do that. But the blood of Christ will. It's as the church has sung for years:

> What can wash away my sin?
> Nothing but the blood of Jesus;
> What can make me whole again?
> Nothing but the blood of Jesus.[26]

You can't escape pain and evil in this life. It's there. I can't even promise you that after giving your life to Jesus Christ there will never be another evil thought of revenge. There probably *will* be! But I can promise that, with Christ in control of your life, you will have some built-in controls that can keep you from carrying out the wishes of your wicked old nature.

Beginning today, you can experience an internal transformation. A simple prayer will do, offered in all sincerity:

> *Heavenly Father, I'm like Haman, in that I live with evil in me, and I have discovered that I cannot conquer it. I believe that Jesus paid the price for my sinfulness, and I believe He rose from the grave and still lives, offering me daily power. And I believe His death paid a penalty I should have paid, but I wasn't qualified to die. So, I take Him into my life now. Thank You, Lord, for invading my life as You once invaded this planet.*

God's grace sees beyond our deepest need. He meets us where we are, talking straight to us in terms that even we can understand. He does this through His Word, even as He has done in this virtually obscure entry from an ancient scroll titled Esther, a story as relevant as Timothy McVeigh's grudge and murderous act of revenge. And because you and I are no better in our inner nature than that convicted murderer, we need God's great grace to clear our hearts of all malice. He can give us the ability to turn our pain over to Him in this life, enabling us to resist all attempts at getting even, while He, through His power, deals with this unsolvable problem for us.

Life and pain may be synonymous, but they do not leave us as helpless victims of our "evil interludes." God and grace are sufficient to change you from a person of wickedness to a person of righteousness. The question is, will you release yourself, by faith, to Him and let Him do that for you?

The only one who can answer that question is you. And not until you answer it with a resounding "Yes!" will you find an escape from your own "evil interludes." If I may propose a brighter side of *The New England Primer:*

> Our days may include much trouble here,
> Our lives lacking power and might.
> But there is hope beyond hatred and fear,
> How great a Savior is Christ![27]

CHAPTER FIVE

Thinking and Saying What's Right—Regardless

I n an overpopulated world, it's easy to underestimate the significance of one. There are so many people who have so many gifts and skills who are already doing so many things that are so important, who needs me? What can I as one individual contribute to the overwhelming needs of our world? Sure is easy to let the vastness of our surroundings do a number on us, isn't it?

But the truth is, you are you—the only you in all the world.

I like the way Edward Everett Hale addresses this point:

> I am only one,
> But still I am one.
> I cannot do everything;
> but still I can do something;
> and because I cannot do everything
> I will not refuse to do the something that I can do.[28]

There is only one you. You're the only person with your exact heritage, your precise series of events in the pilgrimage and sufferings of life that have brought you to this hour. You're the only one with your personal convictions, your makeup, your skills, your appearance, your touch, your voice, your style, your surroundings, your sphere of influence—you're the only one.

THE SIGNIFICANT IMPACT OF ONLY ONE

History is full of accounts of single individuals who have made a difference. Think of the military battles that have turned on the axis of one heroic person. Think of the artists and the contribution of their individual lives, from Michelangelo and da Vinci to Brahms and Beethoven. Think of the scientists, the inventors, the explorers, the technological experts who have literally changed the course of history. Think of the courageous preachers down through time who have stood alone in the gap and made a difference. The face of the church was changed by significant individuals—men like Augustine, Tyndale, Bunyan, Luther, Calvin, Whitefield, Wesley, Edwards, Spurgeon, Moody, and Graham, to name only a few.

Or, to look at it from another angle, think of the difference one vote can make. Come voting time, many neglect to exercise one of the greatest privileges of democracy, thinking that their vote makes no difference. Several years ago I came across a profound statement that conveys the importance of one vote.

- In 1645, one vote gave Oliver Cromwell control of England;
- In 1649, one vote caused Charles I of England to be executed;
- In 1776, one vote gave America the English language instead of German;
- In 1839, one vote elected Marcus Morton governor of Massachusetts;
- In 1845, one vote brought Texas into the Union;
- In 1868, one vote saved President Andrew Johnson from impeachment.
- In 1875, one vote changed France from a monarchy to a republic;
- In 1876, one vote gave Rutherford B. Hayes the United States presidency;

- In 1923, one vote gave Adolph Hitler control of the Nazi party;
- In 1941, one vote saved the Selective Service System just 12 weeks before Pearl Harbor![29]

When I read God's Word, I don't find that many stories about great crusades and city-wide revivals and mass meetings where God's attention rested on an entire country or a whole community. More often, I find individual men and women who made a difference, who set the pace or cut a wide swath or stood in the gap and changed their times. From Genesis to Revelation, we see God's hand on the lives of individuals who thought and said and did what was right—regardless—and as a result, history was made. It was this single observation many years ago that first planted the seed in my mind of writing a series of biblical biographies.

Listen to some verses that declare the importance of one.

> For the eyes of the LORD move to and fro throughout the earth that
> He may strongly support those whose heart [singular] is completely
> His. . . .
>
> 2 Chronicles 16:9

> . . . Now the Lord saw,
> And it was displeasing in His sight that there was no justice.
> And He saw that there was no man,
> And was astonished that there was no one to intercede. . . .
>
> Isaiah 59:15–16

> "Roam to and fro through the streets of Jerusalem,
> And look now, and take note.
> And seek in her open squares,
> If you can find a man,
> If there is *one* who does justice, who seeks truth,
> Then I will pardon her."
>
> Jeremiah 5:1 (emphasis added)

"And I searched for a man among them who should build up the wall and stand in the gap before Me for the land, that I should not destroy it; but I found no one."

Ezekiel 22:30

Only one missionary invests his whole life in an area and a tribe is ultimately evangelized. Only one statesman stands for right and a country is saved. Only one strong-willed and determined citizen says, "I stand against this evil," and a community ramps up morally and changes its direction. And, as we shall see, only one woman decided it was worth the risk to break with protocol and speak her mind , and a nation was preserved. As I stated in the opening words of my introduction, "The power of a woman!"

The Jews have been threatened with extermination. Wicked Haman has influenced King Ahasuerus, with his promises. "Because of this plan I have set up, it is possible for me to pour this money into your treasuries and for us to rid the land of these people who will not bow down and worship you as the king." Though it pandered to the king's pride, that plan had the makings of the worse kind of holocaust. "The Jews will no longer be in our land. We'll be rid of these people."

In case you wonder what impact it had on the community, return to the last phrase in chapter 3: "the city of Susa was in confusion."

While Haman and Ahasuerus sat over their drinks in the palace, the general public wandered in bewilderment and confusion, especially the Jews, not unlike those in the ghetto at Warsaw and other European scenes of horror in the late '30s and early '40s. "What's going on here?" "Why have those in authority ordered this?" "How much worse can things get?"

What terror this struck in their hearts, what fear in their minds! "How can we continue?" "How can we fight this?" This was the law of the Medes and the Persians. When an edict was set forth in that era, it was final. Nobody could change this plan, certainly no Jew. Helplessness eroded into hopelessness.

Yet, in the midst of all this, God was not sleeping. In His sovereign plan, He determined one person would make the difference. Again, one individual would stand in the gap. On this occasion, her name is Esther.

Follow the story as we look first at the response of the people, lost in mourning and weeping.

THE ESSENTIAL INTERVENTION OF QUEEN ESTHER

> When Mordecai learned all that had been done, he tore his clothes,
> put on sackcloth and ashes, and went out into the midst of the city
> and wailed loudly and bitterly.
>
> Esther 4:1

When in bankruptcy or living with a dread disease or having buried a family member or having gone through some terrible disaster in one's city, people in Esther's day would commonly wear loose-fitting, dark-colored coarse garments made of goat's hair, which hung on them like a large gunnysack. On top of that, they would take ashes from the remains of a fire and throw them on themselves so they would be covered with them and appear ghastly and unclean. Sometimes they would even sit in the midst of a cold ash heap and throw the ashes on themselves as a vivid expression of their grief.

People express their sorrow and mourn in different ways. In our Western culture, our expression of grief is often restrained. When President John Kennedy was assassinated, his young widow wore a dark veil as her expression of mourning, hiding her tears behind it. Often, in our culture, people sob quietly, or compassionately hug those who are grieving.

In the East, however, sorrow has always been expressed visibly and vocally. We have all seen pictures of great mobs as they push a casket overhead through the crowd while screaming and crying out. They cry out verses from their sacred word and they claw at the casket. They *wail!* And they *mourn!*

That's what Mordecai does here. He holds nothing back. His grief knows no bounds. In sackcloth and ashes he stumbles toward the gate of the palace.

> And he went as far as the king's gate, for no one was to enter the king's
> gate clothed in sackcloth.
>
> Esther 4:2

Mordecai knew he would not be allowed to enter the king's gate, the gate where the king would come to meet with his subjects and make judgments, according to eastern custom. Perhaps Mordecai went there, making himself visible, hoping to capture the attention of the queen. For it's doubtful that Esther knew much if anything about this edict. She lived in the secluded, highly protected environment of the harem, locked away from the concerns of the common people.

But Susa, the capital, was not the only place where such demonstrations of mourning were taking place.

> And in each and every province where the command and decree of the king came, there was great mourning among the Jews, with fasting, weeping, and wailing; and many lay on sackcloth and ashes.
>
> Esther 4:3

It's a picture of widespread sorrow and loud mourning.

Have you noticed how suffering brings people together? Have you watched how people respond to disasters? I mentioned the trial of Timothy McVeigh earlier. What I didn't mention was the overwhelming response of fellow Americans. Not only the folks from Oklahoma City but people from the rest of the country rallied together after that horrendous bombing. With outpourings of every form of sympathy and compassion, from the rescuers who toiled without rest to those who offered every kind of tangible relief. We've seen the same kind of thing following several airplane disasters. No one was "forced" to respond; they came voluntarily, drawn like magnets to minister to those in need. The same happened in North Dakota following that awful flood in the spring of 1997.

Suffering pushes us out of our homes. It puts us in touch with our neighbors. As my brother, Orville, stated after losing so much when Hurricane Andrew swept across southern Florida, "It blew down all our fences and we finally got to meet all our neighbors!" Hardship forces us to grab hands with one another and pull up closer together. Suffering *never ruined a nation!* Hardship *doesn't fracture families.* Affluence does! But not suffering. Not hardship. It pushes everybody to the same level with the same goal: *survival.*

And so we're not surprised to find these Jews weeping and wailing and fasting together.

> Then Esther's maidens and her eunuchs came and told her, and the queen writhed in great anguish. And she sent garments to clothe Mordecai that he might remove his sackcloth from him, but he did not accept them.
>
> Esther 4:4

"What is happening?" Esther must have thought when she heard of Mordecai's state. "What is going on? Why is he in mourning?" Now that she is a part of the king's household restrained from contact with those outside the palace, Esther cannot speak to Mordecai directly, so she sends him clothing to replace his sackcloth, as a way of offering comfort to him for whatever has happened. But Mordecai refuses the clothing. Esther then sends one of the king's servants to find out the truth from Mordecai.

> Then Esther summoned Hathach from the king's eunuchs, whom the king had appointed to attend her, and ordered him to go to Mordecai to learn what this was and why it was.
>
> So Hathach went out to Mordecai to the city square in front of the king's gate. And Mordecai told him all that had happened to him, and the exact amount of money that Haman had promised to pay to the king's treasuries for the destruction of the Jews. He also gave him a copy of the text of the edict which had been issued in Susa for their destruction, that he might show Esther and inform her; and to order her to go in to the king to implore his favor and to plead with him for her people.
>
> Esther 4:5–8

Mordecai not only informs Esther, through her servant, of all that has happened, even down to the specifies regarding the exact amount of money in the deal; he also sends along official evidence—a copy of the text of the edict. "Have your queen read this," he says. "This was signed with the king's signet ring." He didn't lose control of his emotions; he didn't exaggerate. He was careful with the information he communicated.

Why do I make such a point of this? Because we live in a day of hearsay, when few people pass along information that is precise and reliable. Do you? Are you careful about what you say? Do you have the facts? Do you offer proof that the information you are conveying is correct? While there are occasions when it's appropriate to pass along needed and serious information to the right sources, I'm finding more than ever a growing preoccupation with rumor and slander. Half truths and innuendos become juicy morsels in the mouths of unreliable gossips. There is no way to measure the number of people who have been hurt by rumor and exaggeration and hearsay. Perhaps you have suffered this yourself.

This kind of false information has happened to me several times. I recall being sent a registered letter from a man in which he said, "Tell me when you almost committed suicide. I heard this past week that when you spoke to _____ (he named the group) that you mentioned that you had almost taken your life." Well, the truth of the matter is, I have never almost taken my life. I did remember speaking to the group he mentioned, and in my talk I alluded to some of the strains and difficulties in ministry. Obviously, somebody in the audience read their own exaggerated interpretation into my comments. That's how false rumors get started. It certainly made for a much more dramatic story. But it was an untrue story, and could have been a hurtful and harmful story. Thankfully, he wrote me personally to get the straight scoop. Not all do!

Up in the Northwest, about every two or three years, the rumor resurfaces that I'm divorced. And so rather regularly I have to send word up there that I remain who I've always been, "the husband of one wife"! This is the same woman who's been willing to stay with me for over forty-two years. *That's the amazing thing!*

Be careful what you say. Be careful how you say it. Be careful that you send the right message, and that you send it to the right person, and that you do so with the right motive.

Mordecai correctly covers all those bases. He has some volatile information the queen needs to know. He also knows that he has put the issue on the line for Esther. He has asked her "to go in to the king to implore his favor and plead with him for her people." He knows if she acts on this it could be "curtains" for her. At present, no one in the palace knows she is Jewish. If she believes this information and acts on it, as Mordecai is requesting, she is risking everything, so this is no time for rumor. This is a time for "accuracy in reporting"! James Hastings captures the drama of the moment:

> Mordecai contemplated this bitter necessity. He gazed upon it till his eyes were a fountain of tears. He studied the situation till the iron entered into his very soul. Then he made his appeal to Queen Esther to stand forward as the saviour of her people.[30]

I feel certain that when Mordecai saw Esther's messenger standing there before him, he thought something like this: *This is the moment. This is my only chance. I must get word to Esther. It is her time to stand in the gap.*

> And Hathach came back and related Mordecai's words to Esther. Then Esther spoke to Hathach and ordered him to reply to Mordecai: "All the king's servants and the people of the king's provinces know that for any man or woman who comes to the king to the inner court who is not summoned, he has but one law, that he be put to death, unless the king holds out to him the golden scepter so that he may live. And I have not been summoned to come to the king for these thirty days." And they related Esther's words to Mordecai.
>
> Esther 4:9–12

Now, before you frown and entertain thoughts of self-righteousness, thinking that you would never have responded like that, remember, you're surrounded by friends in a safe and unthreatened environment where there are no armed soldiers outside and governmental protocol to obey. Furthermore, chances are good you don't live under a cloud because of the race into which you were born and there's no king sitting on a throne at whose whim you live or die. It's easy to be brave when we're protected and secure, when we have nothing to risk.

If Esther obeyed Mordecai, she stood to risk everything, including her life. Although the king was her husband, she couldn't just stroll into his office and casually unload what was on her mind. Things didn't work like that in ancient Persia. He had to send for her. And at that time, he hadn't sent for her for a month. If she went to him without being summoned, he could have her put to death. On top of all that, she was Jewish. Who knows how that Gentile monarch would respond when he found that out?

It was a huge dilemma. But Mordecai knew Esther. He had reared her. He had trained her. He knew how far he could push. Most of all, he knew her character. He knew the stuff of which she was made.

Encouraging the cultivation of character is exactly what wise parents do, nudging, urging their children toward maturity. As a parent, you have occasions in your life, brief vignettes, little windows of time, where you can step forward and help your children to understand the value of being brave. As they grow up and those hands-on occasions change to a more distant relationship, you must call upon your children to stand for what they believe, even if they must stand alone—and then trust them to do it without your presence alongside.

Mordecai is at that moment. So when Hathach comes to him with Esther's answer, Mordecai tightens the sash around his sackcloth and says the hard thing. He appeals to her character. I love this moment in the story of Esther! I smile with great delight as I imagine Mordecai's passion as he stated these eloquent words—three significant sentences that, if acted upon, could alter the history of the Jews.

> Then Mordecai told them to reply to Esther, "Do not imagine that you in the king's palace can escape any more than all the Jews. For if you remain silent at this time, relief and deliverance will arise for the Jews from another place and you and your father's house will perish. And who knows whether you have not attained royalty for such a time as this?"
>
> Esther 4:13–14

This goes down in history as one of those "turning point speeches." Mordecai says, "First of all, if you do nothing, don't think you will escape death. Being a Jew, you will die like the rest of us. And second, even if we die, God is not limited to you or me, nor will He allow His people to perish. He will use someone to save our nation. And then, third, how great it would be if He sovereignly chose to use *you*. Could it be that this explains why you were chosen to be queen, my dear Esther—for such a time as this—for this very moment?" This is intrinsic motivation at its best.

Winston Churchill was a master at wording such rallying remarks. In a speech to his beleaguered nation in the House of Commons, June 18, 1940, he said,

> Let us brace ourselves to our duties, and so bear ourselves that if the British Empire and its Commonwealth last for a thousand years, men will still say, "This was their finest hour."

And not quite four months later, in possibly the darkest hour of the war for Great Britain, he said, "Death and sorrow will be the companions of our journey, hardship our garment; constancy our valor and our only shield. We must be *united*, we must be *undaunted*, we must be *inflexible*."

Stand alone! Fight to the end! It's Patrick Henry's, "Give me liberty or give me death." It's Nathan Hale's, "I only regret that I have but one life to lose for my country." It is patriotism standing at attention.

And this is the kind of message Mordecai sends to Esther. "This is your hour. *Stand. Speak! Die!* But whatever you do, *Don't be silent.*" Esther shows her true colors—and they are brilliantly bold. Her words reveal enormous faith mixed with courage:

> "Go, assemble all the Jews who are found in Susa, and fast for me; do not eat or drink for three days, night or day. I and my maidens also will fast in the same way. And thus I will go in to the king, which is not according to the law; and if I perish, I perish."
>
> Esther 4:16

Is that a great answer or what? Is this a great woman? She's had only a few moments to consider what Mordecai had told her, a brief slice of time to weigh his counsel. It was all she needed. She is determined to make a difference, no matter what the consequences to her personally: "If I perish, I perish. If a guard drives a sword through my body, I die doing the right thing." She has changed from fear to abandonment and faith, from hesitation to confidence and determination, from concern for her own safety to concern for her people's survival. She has reached her own personal hour of decision and has not been found wanting.

Do you recall when young David was asked by his father to leave the sheep and take some food and supplies to his brothers who were fighting the Philistines at the valley of Elah? When he got there, he found the giant Goliath roaming the battlefield, taunting and blaspheming the God of Israel. When he learns what is going on, he says, in effect, "Let's do something about it." And his older brother, Eliab, laughs and says sarcastic stuff like, "Oh, so you're going to be the big-time hero, huh? How are all those little woollies doing while you're out here on the battlefield with us?" Remember young David's answer? "Is there not a cause (1 Sam. 17:29 KJV)?" Shortly thereafter he whips out his slingshot and downs Goliath with one smooth stone.

"Of course there is a cause!" David implies, if not in words at least in his actions, "What are you doing sitting around in your tents with your knees knocking? There is a giant out there who hates the cause of the living God! What are you men doing standing here? Our God will fight for me. And if I perish, I perish."

Esther realized the same thing. She realized there was an enemy out there, not only of her people, but more importantly, of the living God. And as soon as that realization seized her awareness, the softness of the palace became uncomfortable.

Eugene Peterson, in his fine book, *Five Smooth Stones for Pastoral Work*, states,

> Wherever there is a people of God there are enemies of God.
> . . . A realization that there is, in fact, an *enemy* forces a reassessment of priorities. . . . The moment Haman surfaced, Esther began to move from being a beauty queen to becoming a Jewish saint, from

being an empty-headed sex symbol to being a passionate intercessor, from the busy-indolent life in the harem to the high-risk venture of speaking for and identifying with God's people.[31]

"Enough of the easy life," said Esther. "It's time to put my name on the line. I am Jewish and I believe in the living God . . . I'm ready to stand alone for my people. And if I perish, I perish."

If Esther had lived later, in the days of Isaac Watts, she could have *paraphrased* his hymn:

> *I am* a soldier of the cross.
> *I am* a follower of the Lamb.
> *I will not* fear to own His cause
> Or blush to speak His name.
>
> *There are* foes for me to face,
> And *I will* stem the flood,
> This vile world is *no* friend to grace,
> To help me on to God![32]

THE PERSONAL INVOLVEMENT OF EACH INDIVIDUAL—INCLUDING YOU

In our overpopulated world, it is easy to underestimate the significance of one. It is easy to underestimate the value of you: your vote, your convictions, your determination to say, "I stand against this."

I was only nine years old when my dad crossed a picket line. It was during World War II, when our country desperately needed the efforts of every factory worker. In the midst of this, the machinist's union had the audacity to go on strike. But my father's national patriotism and love for his family were greater than his loyalty to the union, so he was willing to be called a "scab" (and a host of other insulting obscenities) for his convictions. I remember his driving our '41 Ford into the yard at the end of the day, with a broken windshield and other smashed windows, and eggs running down the side. This left an indelible impression on my nine-year-old mind, and on my eleven-year-old sister and my twelve-year-old brother. We learned that some things are important enough to make us stand alone, even when friends don't understand or coworkers disagree.

What does it matter if I get involved or not? It matters greatly—it matters to your character! Yes, it's true that God has other ways to accomplish His objectives. He has other people He can use. He isn't frustrated or restrained because you and I may be indifferent. But when that happens, we are the losers. When we have been called "for such a time as this," how tragic if we are not there to stand in that hour.

There will be no celestial shout urging you to take a stand. Nor will a flash of lightning awaken you in the midst of your slumber. It doesn't work like that, so don't sit around waiting passively. Numerous needs and issues surround us. They summon us to stand up and be counted. While we will not be able to respond to all of them, the solution is not to respond to *any* of them! So let me ask you: What are you doing to stand up, to stand alone, to answer the call of God in this hour? Allow me to spell out a few issues and needs worth considering.

Are you involved in helping dysfunctional families? How about those who are homeless and hungry? Or those who are addicted to drugs and/or alcohol? What do you do for the orphans and widows? In "such a time as this," what do you stand against and stand for? Do you take a stand against pornography? Do you support any part of the cause of the pro-life movement against abortion? Where do you stand as it relates to the absence of masculinity, the whole extreme feminist movement? What about the horror of sexual abuse that has become so rampant in our society? Or prejudice against other races or nationalities? What about the developmentally disabled? This is an hour of need. Are you there, ready to be salt and light, in such an hour? Is there not a cause?

What do you do to fight crime in your community, the battering of wives or the mistreatment of children? You say, "Well, I don't believe in marching. I don't believe in blocking the way to an abortion clinic." All right. I respect your convictions, but what will you do in place of that?

Have you opened your home to an unwed mother? I'm not suggesting that you do it someone else's way; I'm simply urging: *Do something! Be counted!* In the PTA meetings, stand up and say, "I vote *against* it! I stand for this, against that." If you perish, you perish (but I seriously doubt you'll be martyred). If you are? Big deal: "Absent from the body, at home with the Lord." At least you died for a cause worth fighting for!

Two primary principles emerge from this passage. While they may be easy to read, they aren't easy to apply—but I dare you!

First: *Not until we believe one person can make a difference will we be willing to risk.*

Do you remember the fourth stanza of the hymn, "God of Grace and God of Glory"?

> Set our feet on lofty places,
> Gird our lives that they may be
> Armored with all Christlike graces
> In the fight to set men free.
>
> Grant us wisdom,
> Grant us courage,
> That we fail not man nor Thee,
> That we fail not man nor Thee.[33]

Let me put it straight. Quit being so careful about protecting your own backside. Stop worrying about what others will think. You don't answer to them. You answer to Him. He will help. He will give you wisdom and courage. You may be only one, but you are one. So, risk!

Second: *Only when we move from the safe harbor of theory to the risky world of reality do we actually make a difference.*

It was back in the early 1970s that Cynthia and I first opened our home to an unwed mother. We had four children of our own already (one still in diapers). And our little home was just a bit over 1,000 square feet, so why add to the challenge? The desire for privacy and an ultra-busy schedule could easily have kept us safely removed from the world of reality. And nobody would've said a word. After all, I was a pastor with a growing flock who had needs, too. But we decided we needed to make a difference, and we did. And later we did it again . . . and yet again.

When it comes time to vote, we vote! We don't think about how nice it would be to vote. We don't tell others how they should vote. *We vote!* We vote our conscience. We go to the trouble. Men and women have died that we might have the privilege. When an issue arises and we vote against it, we say by voting, "I stand against that."

You are a thinking citizen, an individual who knows Christ—OK, then, *do something about it!* Say something about it! Stand alone! It's the deed that connects us to reality. It's the deed that moves us from the safe harbor of theory. It's not just the thought, it's the deed! One man writes,

> Grant us the will to fashion as we feel,
> Grant us the strength to labour as we know,
> Grant us the purpose, ribbed and edged with steel,
> To strike the blow.

> Knowledge we ask not—knowledge Thou hast lent,
> But, Lord, the will—there lies our bitter need,
> Give us to build above the deep intent
> The deed, the deed.[34]

We evangelicals are *great* on evangelical theory, *great* on theological theory, *great* on moral theory. But we are not rewarded for our theories. It's the deed! The *deed!* We're rewarded for the deed.

Does one person make a difference? Let me ask you, did Christ? God so loved the world that *He did something*. He didn't select a committee. He didn't theorize how great it would be for someone to come to our rescue. He didn't simply grieve over our waywardness and wring His hands in sorrow. He did something! And, in turn, the Son of God said to God the Father, "I will go." He *did something* about it. And that's why we can be saved. We don't believe in a theory; we believe in the person of Christ, who died and rose again that we might live and make a difference.

The question is not simply, what do you think of Christ? The question is, what have you *done* about what you think? The issue is not so much, how do you feel about the message of the gospel? The issue is, what have you done about the gospel?

What a model is Esther! A woman with courage to match her convictions. But that was then; this is now. Her issues related to the Jews in ancient Persia. Ours are many, related to the end of the twentieth century and the dawn of the twenty-first. But the need is the same—people like you and me who are willing and ready to think, say, and do what is right, regardless.

Are you?

> God of grace and God of glory,
> On Thy people pour Thy power;
> Crown Thine ancient Church's story,
> Bring her bud to glorious flower.
>
> Set our feet on lofty places,
> Gird our lives that they may be
> Armored with all Christlike graces
> In the fight to set men free.
>
> Grant us wisdom,
> Grant us courage,
> That we fail not man nor Thee,
> That we fail not man nor Thee.[35]

CHAPTER SIX

Esther's Finest Hour

When it comes to touching the heart, few things do it as well as a song or a story. We all know occasions where the right music combined with the right lyrics wooed us or someone we know back to God. Sometimes it is a song that our mother taught us, or some moving hymn we learned years ago in church. Nostalgia serves us best when it's a magnet, drawing our heart back to God.

A story will do the same, softening the soil of our souls. When you have the right characters who carry out life's issues in a plot that is mixed with adventure and surprise and some humor, along with purpose and an ultimate moral, there's something about that story that sweeps us into a right state of mind. Esther is just such a story. It has adventure and suspense mixed with enough courage and hope plus a touch of humor and certainly a twist of surprise.

What a great film or play *Esther* would make. Can't you just hear the words of Mordecai ringing with passion as he says, "If you remain silent at this time, relief and deliverance will arise for the Jews from another place and you and your father's house will perish. And who knows whether you have not attained royalty for such a time as this?"

And then, with incredible courage, Esther herself replies, "Go and assemble all the Jews who are found in Susa, and fast for me; do not eat or drink for three days, night or day. I and my maidens also will fast in the same way. And thus I will go to the king, which is not according to law; and if I perish, I perish."

I can hear the applause as the curtain closes on this act with this grand speech that prepares our leading lady to take her place in history.

It reminds me of something C. S. Lewis said about the importance of being loyal to a cause that is greater than ourselves. He likened that quality to a person's chest. "What we need are people with *chests*." The old American word for this is "guts." We need people with guts who will say, "I will stand for this, and if I must die for it, then I die."

It also brings to mind the immortal words of Rudyard Kipling, in his poem "If."

> If you can keep your head when all about you
>> Are others losing theirs and blaming it on you;. . .
>
> If you can dream—and not make dreams your master;
>> If you can think—and not make thoughts your aim;
> If you can meet with triumph and disaster
>> And treat those two impostors just the same; . . .
>
> If you can talk with crowds and keep your virtue,
>> Or walk with kings—nor lose the common touch;
> If neither foes nor loving friends can hurt you;
>> If all men count with you, but not too much; . . .
> Yours is the earth and everything that's in it,
>> And—which is more—You'll be a Man, my son![36]

I love those lines. Stand alone, proclaims Kipling. Be courageous—no matter what the cost.

A long-time friend of mine told me with pride about his twelve-year-old grandson who resigned from delivering the *San Francisco Examiner*. In doing so, this twelve-year-old boy wrote the following letter:

The San Francisco Newspaper Agency
Agent of the *San Francisco Examiner*,
Circulation Department

Gentlemen:

I am a carrier for the *San Francisco Examiner*. As provided in Section 14a of the Youth Carrier Delivery contract, I am giving the newspaper agency a minimum of 30 days written notice prior to my resignation. Please note my resignation will go into effect Tuesday [date]. . . . I am quitting as a form of protest against the series you printed in early June entitled Gay in America and the very unprofessional and biased manner in which you report on touchy subjects like "Gay Liberation" and Abortion issues. I could not in good conscience comply with all the terms of my contract as stated in paragraph three and solicit a paper that I personally disagree with.

Sincerely,

signed[37]

Would you have written that letter? Would you stand alone against an entire company that stands *for* what you stand against? Would you have the guts to do what that twelve-year-old paperboy did?

I'm reminded of another person who took a stand. His name was Martin Luther and the date was April 18, 1521, at the Diet of Worms, where he said, "Here I stand; I can do no other. God help me. Amen." The prelates of the Roman church despised him for his staunch determination and independent spirit. They would have killed him if they could. They had to be content with excommunicating him. Nevertheless, there he stood. God helped him, and he raised the torch that lit the fires of the Protestant Reformation. Would you have done that? Would you have that kind of "guts"?

When Mother Teresa, the compassionate nun of Calcutta, spoke before an audience in sophisticated Washington D.C., she addressed a deep concern of hers: the abortion issue. As our pro-abortion president sat behind her, she boldly announced, "Send *me* your babies!" Again, it was her "guts" we admired. Would you have the guts to say what she said? That's why we admire Esther. She not only says she will do something; she does it, not knowing if she will live to see another sunrise.

A SILENT YET ELOQUENT INTERLUDE

Between chapters 4 and 5 of this ancient Book of Esther, I find nothing but white space in my Bible, as I'm sure there is in yours. It's a break in time. It's a space of suspense when we don't know what is happening. Nothing is recorded for us to read. We left Esther just as she had sent word to Mordecai that she was going to enter the king's presence uninvited, which could mean her instant death. Then there is a grand pause, and we pick up the story again at the moment, three days later, when Esther is preparing to walk into the presence of the king, not knowing what the future holds. She literally breaks the law of the land by voluntarily interrupting the king.

This space represents a silent yet powerful interlude during which Esther draws on the source of her strength. How easy it is for us to forget that source. How easy for us to believe that she was born with a Mother Teresa conscience and a Joan of Arc courage. Yet just as no one is born prejudiced, so no one is born courageous.

Allow me a moment to pause here and ask you a couple of very personal questions. Do you teach your children to stand up for what they believe? Are you teaching your grandchildren how to be people of character, regardless? That is the way they will learn it. Let me probe one question deeper. Are you modeling authentic character? That leaves the message permanently etched in their minds.

You see, Esther did not come onto this earth with a sensitive conscience and a courageous heart. She learned it from her cousin, who became her mentor and adoptive father, Mordecai. He knew how far he could stretch her with his challenge. And she rose to the challenge and said, "I'll do exactly as you have taught me to do."

But remember what else she said, "Assemble all the Jews in Susa, and have them fast for three days. My handmaidens and I will do the same. After that, I will go to the king."

This implies that during this time of fasting, she would also be waiting on her Lord in prayer. That's what fasting is all about. The Jews didn't stop eating to lose weight; they fasted for spiritual reasons. When an issue this prominent became their concern, it was no time for fun and feasting. Things got pretty intense as they filled the time they would normally spend preparing and consuming food, in protracted periods of prayer and quiet fasting.

So Esther challenged Mordecai to round up as many of God's people as he could find in the streets of Susa and have them fast and pray for her. She was saying, "Pray for me. Fast for me. And my maidens and I will do the same. And we will see what God will do." In other words, she determined to wait on the Lord and allow Him to guide her thoughts and help her frame her words.

Now even though there's white space between these two chapters, don't think for a moment that God is whiling away His time, busy with other things. Remember, He may be invisible, but He is at work. That's the beauty of His invisibility. He can be moving in a thousand places at the same time, working in circumstances that are beyond our control. During a waiting period, God is not only working in our hearts, He's working in others' hearts. And all the while He is giving added strength. Remember Isaiah's words about waiting?

> Yet those who wait for the LORD
> Will gain new strength;
> They will mount up with wings like eagles,
> They will run and not get tired,
> They will walk and not become weary.
>
> Isaiah 40:31

Even though the prophet's pen put these words on the sacred page centuries ago, that verse of Scripture is as pertinent and relevant as what you read in the paper this morning—and far more trustworthy.

From this verse we learn that four things happen when we wait:

First, *we gain new strength.* We may feel weak, even intimidated, when we turn to our Lord. While waiting, amazingly, we exchange our weakness for His strength.

Second, *we get a better perspective.* It says we "will mount up with wings like eagles." Eagles can spot fish in a lake several miles away on a clear day. By soaring like eagles while waiting, we gain perspective on what we are dealing with.

Third, *we store up extra energy.* "We will run and not get tired." Notice, it's future tense. When we do encounter the thing we have been dreading, we will encounter it with new strength—extra energy will be ours to use.

Fourth, *we will deepen our determination to persevere.* We "will walk and not become weary." The Lord whispers reassurance to us. He puts steel in our bones, so to speak. We begin to feel increasingly more invincible.

We'll gain new strength. We'll get better perspective. We'll store up extra energy. We'll deepen our determination to persevere. All that happens when we wait.

And at the same time, during that period of waiting, nothing is happening—at least nothing visible. You could easily tell yourself at the time, *I'm waiting in vain. Nothing's going to change.* That's what the adversary wants you to think: "Waiting's a waste."

Don't you believe it! When the enemy's message roams into your mind, you need to kick it out. Reject it. Look at another verse in Isaiah, just a few verses after the "eagle" verse.

> "Do not fear, for I am with you;
> Do not anxiously look about you, for I am your God.
> I will strengthen you, surely I will help you,
> Surely I will uphold you with My righteous right hand."
>
> "For I am the Lord your God, who upholds your
>   right hand,
> Who says to you, 'Do not fear, I will help you.'"
>
> Isaiah 41:10,13

It's those kinds of thoughts that strengthened Esther while she was waiting and praying and fasting three days.

Mordecai did the same, as Esther had commanded. Now the roles were reversed. He was no longer in charge; she was. Or, better still, the Lord was. And as the Lord gripped her heart, she became unafraid of what she faced. It was a silent yet powerful parenthesis in Esther's life.

This may be one of those "white spaces" in your own life. Maybe it's time for you to pray and to fast and to call upon a few close friends to fast and pray with you. Maybe it's time for you to say, "I'm not going to rush into this unpredictable and unprecedented situation. I don't know my way through. I can't find the path to walk. So I'm going to wait. In the meantime, I'm going to give it to God. I'm going to listen with a sensitive ear. I'm going to watch the Lord's leading with a sensitive eye." I'm reminded of the psalmist's words:

> Therefore, let everyone who is godly pray to Thee in a time
>   when Thou mayest be found;
> Surely in a flood of great waters they shall not reach him.
> Thou art my hiding place; Thou dost preserve me from trouble;
> Thou dost surround me with songs of deliverance.
>
> Psalm 32:6–7

And God answers,

> I will instruct you and teach you in the way which you should go;
> I will counsel you with My eye upon you.
>
> Psalm 32:8

God counsels us with His eye. The eye makes no sound when it moves. It requires a sensitive earthly eye to watch the movement of the eye of God—God's directions. All He may do is turn your attention in another direction. But that's all you may need. When you wait, you listen. You pore over a favorite passage in His Word. You quietly give attention to His presence and to His direction. I'm suggesting that that's precisely what happens during the interlude between these two chapters in Esther's life.

As she prepares for her finest hour, she must wait, think, pray, stay quiet, fast, and listen in her soul.

A CALM, WISE, CONFIDENT PLAN

Because of this interlude with God, Esther is able to approach the moment of truth—to step into the presence of the king—calmly and wisely and confidently.

> Now it came about on the third day that Esther put on her royal robes and stood in the inner court of the king's palace in front of the king's rooms, and the king was sitting on his royal throne in the throne room, opposite the entrance to the palace. And it happened when the king saw Esther the queen standing in the court, she obtained favor in his sight; and the king extended to Esther the golden scepter which was in his hand. So Esther came near and touched the top of the scepter.
>
> Esther 5:1–2

In the margin beside that verse in your Bible, I'd like you to write a verse from the Proverbs that I mentioned in a previous chapter.

> The king's heart is like channels of water in the hand of the LORD;
> He turns it wherever He wishes.
>
> Proverbs 21:1

No king has ever intimidated God, no matter how wealthy his treasury, how extensive his kingdom, or how powerful his armies. God can handle anyone. *Anyone!* He can handle your husband. He can handle your wife. He can handle your kids. He can handle your pastor. He can handle the person who gives you grief. He can handle your ex-mate, that person who made you all those promises and broke most of them. He can even handle your enemy. He can handle the most intimidating situation, because in the hand of the Lord, any heart is like water.

jolted by them. Too many Christians are lulled into languor. Some can warble all the Christian songs, and recite all the right Bible verses, and quote this preacher and that teacher, but their Christian lives, down deep inside, are jaded. Are you in that condition? When that happens, you become calloused and insensitive, and you're in for a life of boredom and mediocrity. How tragic for that to happen! The walk of faith is designed to be a walk of adventure, filled with periodic and delightful surprises.

Some Christians become like the people who once greeted President Theodore Roosevelt at a gala ball. All of them said the same thing, smiled the same tired smile, repeating the right greetings by rote, talking with their mouths, not their heads or their hearts. Tired of shaking hands and smiling his big smile and responding with the usual inanities used at such occasions, Roosevelt did something absolutely outrageous. Convinced that no one was listening anyway, he began to greet the rest of his guests by saying with a smile, "I murdered my grandmother this morning." Everyone smiled vacuously and said things like: "Wonderful!" "Lovely!" "Keep up the good work!" One diplomat was listening, however. He leaned over and whispered in Roosevelt's ear, "I'm sure she had it coming to her!"[38]

Empty Christian talk drives me up a wall when it is filled with clichés and bromides. Doesn't nonsensical small talk make you want to throw up? Especially when you realize you have been guilty of it yourself. The more it goes on in our lives, the more the *real* Christian life is losing its zip.

With Esther, her walk with God was an exciting adventure. She stepped into the king's presence because she had confidence in God. Esther planned a banquet because she trusted God to do the unexpected. Are you still open to the unexpected? Are you really waiting on the Lord to do His will?

Let's say you're single and you really want to be married. And you're waiting on the Lord to do . . . what? Find you a mate? But are you ready for Him to say, "Surprise! You will find happiness in being single for the rest of your life"?

You may be married and having serious trouble with your mate. And so you wait on the Lord to take care of him. Take care of her. But during the waiting period the Lord says, "Surprise! We have to take care of you. You're a greater part of the problem than your mate."

Perhaps you are a parent of a wayward child. Are you ready to hear, "Surprise! You're part of the reason your child is such a rebel"?

Or you may finally feel settled. Happy in your job and somewhat financially secure. But soon, God may be saying to you, "Surprise! I'm going to move you out of this job, away from this location." Are you willing to shift agendas for God to have His way?

Who would ever have guessed God's plan for Esther? Yet here she was, at the banquet with the king and Haman. By the way, she still hasn't told the king what is troubling her, but surely he knows something is wrong. She would never have risked coming into his presence as she did unless she had a very good reason. So as they're sitting together at the feast, he raises the matter again.

> And, as they drank their wine at the banquet, the king said to Esther, "What is your petition, for it shall be granted to you. And what is your request? Even to half of the kingdom it shall be done."
>
> So Esther answered and said, "My petition and my request is: if I have found favor in the sight of the king, and if it please the king to grant my petition and do what I request, may the king and Haman come to the banquet which I shall prepare for them, and tomorrow I will do as the king says."
>
> Esther 5:6–8

Esther could have done everything today that she's going to do tomorrow, but she's trusting God's timing on this. So she says, "There's something I do want to say to you, but I want to wait till tomorrow." For some reason, as we'll soon learn, God's timing requires one more day.

A PROUD AND SINISTER RESPONSE

Meanwhile, Haman, the guy you love to hate, is strutting around Cloud Nine.

> Then Haman went out that day glad and pleased of heart; but when Haman saw Mordecai in the king's gate, and that he did not stand up

or tremble before him, Haman was filled with anger against Mordecai.
Haman controlled himself, however, went to his house, and sent for
his friends and his wife Zeresh.

Esther 5:9–10

He walks out of the palace thinking, *Boy, am I ever in clover. I've just had a private dinner and audience with the king and the queen. What an honor. My star is on the rise. The sky's the limit.* It was the ultimate opportunity to drop names. Can you imagine Haman at the office the next day? "I was with the king and queen last night, and—yeah, a banquet for just the three of us. Yes, I was the only one invited. As expected, I received a personal invitation from the queen."

So he walks out of the palace, bursting with pride and ego, and he runs into Mordecai—that Jew who *will not respect him.*

I love Mordecai. He's on top of everything, in the exact place where he should be for his part in God's plan. Remember, the last time we saw him he couldn't go into the king's gate because he was wearing sackcloth and ashes. But now here he is, in the king's gate. Obviously he's changed clothes. He senses God's at work. He knows that something great is about to happen. Also, despite Haman's official status and power, despite his evil decree, Mordecai is still not intimidated by Haman. He knows his God is greater than Haman. So when Haman walks out of the palace, Mordecai doesn't look at all impressed.

Again, Haman is furious. But this time he bites his tongue and heads for home. Mordecai will get his. For now, Haman wants to revel in his own glory. He sends for his wife and his friends.

Then Haman recounted to them the glory of his riches, and the number
of his sons, and every instance where the king had magnified him, and
how he had promoted him above the princes and the servants of the king.

Esther 5:11

Ah, yes. The typical blowhard. Ya-da, ya-da, ya-da. Brag, brag, brag.
Me, me, me. Can you imagine having to sit and listen to this blow-hard?

Of course nobody wants to offend him, because he's the guy with the king's seal. But you know they have to be rolling their eyes and wondering, *How long before we can get out of here?*

He tells them what he's worth. And then he begins bragging about how many sons he has. (A Jewish Targum says, "Haman had 208 other sons, in addition to his own 10." That's another story, no need to get into it.) And then he recounts instance after instance where he has been promoted and exalted. Arrogance ad infinitum, conceit ad nauseam.

Interesting point, though. With all this glory and wealth and power that Haman has, you would think he'd be satisfied. But people like this are *never* satisfied. And what he's not satisfied about at the moment is the fact that Mordecai, one man—one Jew(!)—won't respect him. A person like this wants *everybody* to bow to him. And if one doesn't, this becomes his sole worry and focus.

> Haman also said, "Even Esther the queen let no one but me come with the king to the banquet which she had prepared; and tomorrow also I am invited by her with the king. Yet all of this doesn't satisfy me every time I see Mordecai the Jew sitting at the king's gate."
>
> Esther 5:12-13

Finally his wife pipes up and says, in effect, "So why don't you do something about it? I'm sick and tired of hearing you grouse about this guy Mordecai."

> Then Zeresh his wife and all his friends said to him, "Have a gallows fifty cubits high made and in the morning ask the king to have Mordecai hanged on it, then go joyfully with the king to the banquet." And the advice pleased Haman, so he had the gallows made.
>
> Esther 5:14

Wonderful! Haman loves the idea, and he orders a gallows built fifty cubits high. That's 75 feet. Now, I'd call that overreacting, wouldn't you? That's seven-and-a-half stories. And it doesn't mean "gallows" as we traditionally think of it, pictured in some Western "hang 'em high" movie. The original word here means "tree" or, literally, "pole" or "stake." Remember, in Persia, they didn't hang their victims with a rope; they impaled them. A stake was thrust into the body, and then the body was hung on a pole (in this case seven-and-half stories high). The Romans got the idea of crucifixion from the Phoenicians who earlier learned it from the Persians. That's why Jesus is said to have hung on a tree or on a pole. The Romans developed the practice of driving nails into the hands. But the Persians simply impaled the body on a pole. It was an anguishing, humiliating, torturous death.

Haman's hatred now consumed him, to the point where only the death, the agonizing death, of his enemy would satisfy him. He went to sleep that night listening to the thump and the bump and the pounding of the construction crew as they worked through the night, building the pole upon which his enemy would hang.

SOME DIRECT AND TIMELY ADVICE

We're in the midst of a suspenseful plot, which leads to an amazing turn of events we'll consider in the next chapter, but this is a good place to pause and give thought to how these things we've considered tie in with our lives today.

The longer I think about it, the more obvious are four principles for dealing with difficult situations.

First: *When preparing for an unprecedented event, wait on the Lord before getting involved.* At least as important as the thing we are waiting for is the work God does in us while we wait. He works on our patience. He works on our circumstances. He works on others. If we plunge in, if we run ahead, we foul up His better arrangements and plans.

If you're on the verge of a big decision, wait. In fact, I've found the bigger the decision, the longer the wait. Don't get in a hurry. Especially if it's unprecedented. If you have to cut a new path, if you're walking a road you've never walked before, and there's no map, better wait. Better wait for the Lord. How long? I have no idea. Could be three days, could be three weeks, could be three months. I've waited much longer than that, frankly.

And I should add that during the waiting period, don't try to take things in your own hands. Restrain your tendency to "move things along."

Second: *When dealing with an unpredictable person, count on the Lord to open doors and hearts.* If I may personalize the proverb: When your ways please the Lord, He makes even your enemies to be at peace with you (Prov. 16:7). Count on the Lord to do that.

Amazing things happen to our courage while we're waiting. Rather than getting more fearful, we become less fearful. Rather than losing heart, we gain confidence. The Lord becomes more important. His presence over-shadows the threatening, even intimidating, circumstances that would otherwise immobilize us or paralyze our thoughts.

Third: *When working through an unpleasant situation, trust the Lord for enduring patience.* Think of the patience Esther must have had to refrain from telling the king about Haman, when she had him in the very palm of her hand. Haman, the man who hated her people so much that he was going to have them wiped from the face of the earth. Think of the patience she had to wait for just the right time.

In situations that are unpleasant, timing is as important as action, sometime more so. Pace yourself. Have patience. Wait for the situation to become bearable and workable.

Fourth: *When standing against an unprincipled enemy, ask the Lord for invincible courage.* I believe that's what happened to Esther in the midst of that first banquet. She sensed a growing invincibility and courage, even in the presence of her mortal enemy, as she waited for the Lord's timing. Ask the Lord for that kind of invincible courage. He will grant your request. He will give you the courage to stand.

I said earlier that nothing touches the heart like a song or a story. And the one to whom we sing more songs than to any other person is Jesus Christ. There are more songs composed about the person of Jesus Christ than about any other human being who ever lived. Why? Because His story is like none other.

Did you know that they put Him on a pole, that they hung Him up to die? Did you know that more people hated Him than loved Him? Do you know that more cheered than wept? Do you know that when He died more applauded than sighed? Despised and hated by men and women, He died. Why do we sing to Him then? Because like no other person who has died, He arose from the grave. He is alive today, and He gives *us* a song.

Do you know why He died? Not because some Haman hated Him and decided to put Him on a pole. He died because you and I are sinners. And the only way to satisfy the demand of a holy God in dealing with humanity was to pay the penalty for sin. And that required the price of blood from the unspotted Lamb of God, Jesus Himself.

Perhaps a prayer would be the best way to end a chapter so full of emotion—so personally relevant. And since we've reached the half-way point of the book, it's a good time to pause before God:

> *Father, thank You for giving some of us courage to continue to wait, while at the same time the determination to stand alone, even if it means enduring personal loss and public misunderstanding. Thank You for modern-day Esthers, women and men alike, who have stood up to be counted. They model for us what the Christian life is all about.*
>
> *And, Father, I pray for anyone who, like Haman, has blamed others for his unhappiness and deserves the very gallows upon which he would place his Mordecai. Bring us to an end of our blaming. Bring us to an end of our impatience. Bring us to an end of our arrogance. In doing so, bring us face to face with the claims of Jesus Christ and an acknowledgment of His right to rule in our lives.*
>
> *For all I know, Lord, there are some who read my words today who find themselves in difficult straits. Maybe there's a Haman giving them grief—or a threatening situation that's got them worried and harried. Just as you honored Esther for waiting then acting in wisdom and calm confidence, encourage us to wait on You to work things out—to take control— to give us hope beyond the current chaos.*
>
> *Esther experienced her finest hour when things seemed most unsure. If You could do that for her back then, it isn't out of the question to think you can do that for us today. So, that's what I pray for on behalf of others. Step into our world. Change hearts we cannot budge. Replace our weakness with*

Your strength. Give us a calm and quiet confidence that all things are in Your hands and therefore under control.

Help us to wait patiently for you to work.

In the dear name of Christ. Amen.

Chapter Seven

What Goes Around Comes Around

Things are seldom what they seem. Parents of small children can attest to this. It's when the kids get very quiet and you think all is well that you have something to worry about. Probably there isn't a parent reading this who has not, in one of those quiet lulls, done a quick investigation only to find their two-year-old standing waist-deep in toilet tissue. Or, in our case, ankle-deep in bath powder, with all of the file drawers pulled out and the files folders all over the floor, being doused carefully with a quarter of an inch of bath powder!

One of our friends tells of the time he and his wife were in a large department store with their daughter, and the child somehow got away from them. Immediately upon realizing this, they began a frantic search. Happily, she wasn't far away. As they hurriedly walked up, she was sitting with her back to them. They were so relieved to find her, they decided not to frighten her by grabbing her in their arms. Instead they both leaned over to look into her sweet face, and as they reached down to pick her up, they discovered that all the while she had been chewing on an old cigar butt she had picked up from the floor.

Things are seldom what they seem.

Related to this is a second axiom: When things go wrong, it may seem like they cannot possibly get any worse; but they often do. About the time you think things are as bad as they're going to get, they get even worse.

This was certainly true for a poor guy named Johnson. All of his adult life he had made wrong decisions. Every choice he made was a wrong choice. If he bet on a horse, it would lose every time. If he chose one elevator over another, that would be the elevator that got stuck. If he selected a particular line in the bank, that line would always be the slowest. If he picked a day for a picnic, that would be the day of the cloudburst.

Well, one day it became necessary for this fellow to travel about a thousand miles away from home, and he had to get there in a hurry. The only way to get there was by airplane. The thought frightened him. But to his delight he discovered that only one airline serviced that particular city, so he breathed a sigh of relief. He didn't have to choose. Imagine his horror, then, when he looked out the window after they had been flying for about thirty minutes, and he saw the engine on fire. Being a Catholic, he selected his favorite saint, Saint Francis, and he said, "I have never in my life made the right choice. Why, I don't know. But I have borne my cross without complaint. On this occasion I made no choice. This was the only plane I could have taken, and now it's going down. Why am I being punished?"

Right about then a great hand reached out of the clouds and swept into the plane and pulled him out and held him about two miles above the earth as the plane crashed below. And a great voice echoed, "My son, I can save you, if in truth you have called upon me!" The man cried, "Yes, I have. I've truly called upon you, Saint Francis." "Ah," said the voice, "Saint Francis *Xavier* or Saint Francis of *Assisi?*"

So much for jokes! Let me recount a *true* story I heard about two attorneys from the San Francisco area. Their offices were located far above the ground floor, and they were there at work when an earthquake stuck—a 7.1 quake. Everything went dark as pandemonium broke over the scene. Thankfully, they made their way down to the main floor and out of the building. Once there, they were unable to get to their cars. Transportation was at a standstill. After hours of waiting they finally caught a bus that

discovery of yours caused someone else to be promoted to a place of significance, and now that person has all the glory, the status, the salary, the celebrity and you've never even been recognized, to say nothing of thanked, or rewarded? Have you done the hard thing, the courageous thing, and seen someone else get the credit? Has someone else taken or been given the glory that is rightfully yours?

Learn a lesson from Mordecai today, will you? Through all that happens to him, Mordecai never becomes a man of vengeance. He never tries to get back at Haman, even when he has the opportunity, even when he has Haman in a very vulnerable spot. He doesn't kick him in the face when he has a chance to do so. He doesn't even speak against the man.

Let me challenge you to guard your heart as Mordecai did. And let me encourage you with a verse from the pen of another of the saints of God:

> For God is not unjust so as to forget your work and the love which you have shown toward His name, in having ministered and still ministering to the saints.
>
> Hebrews 6:10

I love those words, "God is not unjust so as to forget." When no one else notices, mark it down, *God notices.* When no one else remembers, God records. The psalmist tells us that He even keeps our tears in a bottle (Ps. 56:8). He will reward us for acts that are done in His name. So be encouraged. There will come a day when rewards will come your way as they should, perhaps not on this earth as happens to Mordecai, but someday. "Weeping may last for the night, but a shout of joy comes in the morning" (Ps. 30:5). God is not unjust so as to forget your work, your labor, your behind-the-scenes contributions.

Third: *When everything seems great, it's not.* Sounds like one of Murphy's Laws, doesn't it? Any time things appear to be going great, you'd better see what's around the next corner. Too bad Haman didn't know about that principle! Perhaps he knew about it, but his conceit fogged his memory.

As soon as the king heard that nothing had been done for Mordecai, his wheels started turning. He began to imagine what might be done to reward this man for his great deed. Then he had to figure out who would help him carry it out. And so he asked the logical question.

> So the king said, "Who is in the court?" Now Haman had just entered the outer court of the king's palace in order to speak to the king about hanging Mordecai on the gallows which he had prepared for him.
> And the king's servants said to him, "Behold, Haman is standing in the court." And the king said, "Let him come in."
>
> Esther 6:4–5

Is this a great moment or what? The sun is barely over the horizon, and here comes Haman, rushing to the palace as early as he can so he will be the first to have an audience with the king and finish off his hated enemy.

Suddenly, out of the inner court, comes the voice of the king, "Call him in. Call Haman in." The king is calling for him. This will be even easier than he anticipated.

Now is my chance, he thinks. He glances out the window with a sinister sneer, *Just a minute, gallows, somebody will be on you*. And with the stride of a peacock he struts into the court of the king.

Before he can get a line out of his mouth, however, the king fills his ears with unexpected words.

> So Haman came in and the king said to him, "What is to be done for the man whom the king desires to honor?" And Haman said to himself, "Whom would the king desire to honor more than me?"
>
> Esther 6:6

When the king asks the question, who does Haman immediately think of? Himself, of course. Who else? This is the guy who carries around four cartridges of slides about his own promotion and shows them every chance he gets. This is the guy who talks about how much money he makes, how many kids he has, how necessary he is to the king, how important he is. Who else would the king want to honor but him? *This is my moment*, he gloats. *So let's see, what could be done for me?* He quickly begins to list every glory he can imagine for himself.

> Then Haman said to the king, "For the man whom the king desires to honor, let them bring a royal robe which the king has worn, and the horse on which the king has ridden, and on whose head a royal crown has been placed; and let the robe and the horse be handed over to one of the king's most noble princes and let them array the man whom the king desires to honor and lead him on horseback through the city square, and proclaim before him, 'Thus it shall be done to the man whom the king desires to honor.'"
>
> Esther 6:7–9

"Great idea," says the king. "Couldn't have thought of something as imaginative. That's terrific, Haman."

Now comes one of my all-time favorite verses.

> Then the king said to Haman, "Take quickly the robes and the horse as you have said, and do so for Mordecai the Jew, who is sitting at the king's gate; do not fall short in anything of all that you have said."
>
> Esther 6:10

Oh, man! This has got to be a mistake, thinks Haman. *The king couldn't possibly have said that hated name, could he? What's happening here?*

"Now I want the finest prince in the kingdom to make the announcement. So, Haman, I want *you* to be the one who leads the horse through the city and makes the announcement about how great this man is who sits on this horse."

Talk about an in-your-face assignment! It had humiliation written all over it. I can't think of a more deflating command to obey than this one. In fact, we can only imagine the tight-lipped, sour attitude of Haman as he carried out the king's wishes. Try not to smile as you imagine the following scene.

So Haman took the robe and the horse, and arrayed Mordecai, and led him on horseback through the city square, and proclaimed before him, "Thus it shall be done to the man whom the king desires to honor."

Esther 6:11

One wise commentator has said, "The words Haman had to proclaim must have been as gravel in his mouth."[39]

What goes around comes around. That popular saying has never been truer than it is here. Things have *gone* around for Haman—yet they finally *come* around for Mordecai. Sitting on that horse in regal attire, he was the most surprised man in the kingdom. That's the beauty of the story. He was not a proud man. He was not a vengeful man. He was not whispering, "Say it a little louder. Eat your heart out, Haman." According to what is written here, Mordecai didn't utter a word.

I think that's what I appreciate most in this whole episode: The silence of Mordecai. How rare are the people who can be promoted to a place of highly visible significance and not live for their own clippings or crave the spotlight or demand center stage. Soft-spoken, genuinely humble celebrities are extremely rare. Not convinced? Check the rank and file of today's pro athletes. How refreshing (and unusual!) to find a modern-day Mordecai!

In fact, the next thing we read is that "Mordecai returned to the king's gate." A brief phrase, easy to overlook. But isn't it wonderful? "Mordecai returned to the king's gate," it says, rather than, "Mordecai decided it was time for a major promotion." And do you know why it's significant? Because that's where he's been all the time. His role has not gone to his head.

In an old book, published back in 1880, I found this insightful comment from a man named Alexander Raleigh:

A proud ambitious man would have said to himself, "No more of the king's gate for me! I shall direct my steps now to the king's palace, and hold myself ready for honour . . . which surely must now be at hand." Mordecai seems to have said with himself, "If these things are designed for me in God's good providence, they will find me. But they must seek me, for I shall not seek them. Those who confer them know my address: 'Mordecai, at the king's gate,' will still find me. Let the crowd wonder and disperse. I have had enough of their incense. Let Haman go whither he will, he is in the hands of the Lord. Let my friends at home wait; they will all hear all in time . . . I can wait best at the old place and in the accustomed way—AT THE KING'S GATE.'"[40]

This is a good place for me to pause and probe. Have you recently been promoted? Has God's providence smiled on you so that your name is now honored in circles where you were once not even known? Have you come to a place of popularity and prosperity? Are you now esteemed in the eyes of others? If so, the real question is: Are you still comfortable at the king's gate, or must you now live at the palace? Must you now be treated with special care and be given kid-glove treatment and not bothered with everyday problems? Mordecai shrugged, "Just drop me off where all this started—at the king's gate."

No matter what happens to you, remember "the pit from which you've been dug." You'll find the best place on earth is still pretty close to your roots. Like the country-western song reminds us, "Look how far I had to come, to get back where I started from. . . ."

Four: *When nothing seems just, it is.* If you're like me, you're often waiting for the other shoe to fall. In this instance, we're waiting for—and wanting—Haman to get what he deserves. Everything within us craves justice. And especially with a loser like Haman, who has strutted his stuff long enough.

> Then Mordecai returned to the king's gate. But Haman hurried home, mourning, with his head covered. And Haman recounted to Zeresh his wife and all his friends everything that had happened to him. . . .
> Esther 6:12–13a

Remember, the last time Haman went home, he was crowing, bragging about how great he was. Now he slides under the door, sniveling and whining about what has happened to him.

The Haman types always blame other people for their misfortune. Have you noticed that? It's never, "God has taught me a valuable lesson" or, "I have been humbled through this" or, "Through this loss I have gained" or, "God has crushed my spirit, but thankfully, I've learned to rely on Him." Instead, invariably, it is, "If it hadn't been for him . . .," "If she hadn't said . . .," "If that person hadn't done . . .," "If the company hadn't . . .," and on and on and on. Haman's like that. He rehearses all that has happened *to* him, not a word about what he brought on himself.

> . . . Then his wise men and Zeresh his wife said to him, "If Mordecai, before whom you have begun to fall, is of Jewish origin, you will not overcome him, but will surely fall before him."
>
> Esther 6:13

You've got to admire their theology. They are right on target. It sounds like a statement straight from Genesis.

> And I will make you [the Jews] a great nation,
> And I will bless you,
> And make your name great;
> And so you shall be a blessing;
> And I will bless those who bless you,
> And the one who curses you I will curse. . . .
>
> Genesis 12:2–3

The marginal reference for these verses states, "I will bind under a curse." In today's terms, this Abrahamic covenant promises: "My people will be protected. You curse them, and you'll pay a terrible price."

Never once in all of Haman's peacock strutting and evil plotting had God ignored him or his plan to murder Mordecai and the Jews. God had not missed his statements, the pride of his heart, the violent and prejudicial motives behind his decisions. God was invisible, but He was not out of touch or passive. He had not forgotten His people or His promises to them—and to their enemies.

While they were still talking with him, the king's eunuchs arrived and hastily brought Haman to the banquet which Esther had prepared.

Esther 6:14

A knock came at the door. And before he could even get his thoughts together, Haman was swept out of the house and escorted to the palace for the banquet that would spell his doom. I can't help but wonder if on the way to the palace Haman glanced again at the gallows he had built for Mordecai, shook his head, and regretted what he had done.

It's the kind of thought Judas had too late, as reflected in an old English couplet:

> Still as of old
> Men by themselves are priced—
> For thirty pieces Judas sold
> Himself, not Christ.[41]

THE MOST SIGNIFICANT PRINCIPLE OF ALL

What goes around comes around.

That saying reminds me of a magnificent theological principle underscored again and again in the Scriptures: *When God seems absent, He's present.* Even when you think you have lost *all,* God uses it as an opportunity to awaken you to the realization He is still in charge, as well as to bring you to your knees.

All this reminds me of the story of a man who was shipwrecked on an uninhabited island. He painstakingly built a little hut for protection from the elements and where he could keep the few items he had salvaged from the wreck. For weeks he lived with only the hot sun and the cold nights and the tropical storms for company. Prayerfully, he scanned the horizon for the approach of a ship. Nothing.

Then, one evening, when he returned from a search for food, he was terrified to find that his little hut was in flames. As he stood there, unable to put out the fire, he was crushed by the disaster. What few possessions he had were now gone up in smoke. He went to sleep that night near the ashes, listening to the surf pounding on the sand and despair throbbing in his heart.

Early the next morning he awoke to find a ship anchored off the island— the first ship he had seen in all the weeks he had been searching for the hope of rescue. Still trying to believe his eyes, he heard footsteps and then heard the captain's voice: "We saw your smoke signal, and we came to rescue you."[42]

Everything the marooned man owned had to be destroyed before he could be discovered—and rescued. God seemed so distant for so long, but He was working on both ends—to bring the ship of rescue near at just the right time and to reduce the marooned man to nothing in order to bring him to his knees.

Where are you in that story? Have you been building your kingdom and amassing your fortune, establishing your name, making it prominent so that other people will ooh and aah? Can you see it in your sights? Have you've walked over and through people to get there?

Do you feel that God has been absent or on hold in your life, distant in some way? I want to close this chapter by reminding you of this: He may have seemed absent from you, but He has been present all along. Furthermore, He knows your heart. He knows the true condition of your soul. He knows the hidden impurities of your motives. He knows the deep depravity of your sin. But He's heard your signal and He will not turn you away.

In the final analysis, God will have His way. He's not impressed with earthly kingdoms and personal towers, with pride and prestige and wealth and fame. He's impressed with a humble heart that comes to Him on His terms. Mordecai and Esther knew this. Haman never learned it. But my concern today is not with them, it's with you. However, there is nothing I can write that will force you to your knees. That's God's job—and He is awfully good at it! He's never turned His back on anyone who truly comes to Him by way of the cross.

Have you? If not, will you? He's available when you're ready. But don't put it off. You can strut around like Haman only so long. Too long! Remember, what goes around comes around.

Chapter Eight

God's Surprising Sovereignty

I've never met a person who didn't feel pity for Job. Here was a man godly in heart and righteous in life who had his entire world crash in on top of him for no apparent reason other than what some might view as a kind of "cosmic joke": satanic cruelty and God's strange allowing of it to happen. The first part we can handle; it's the second part that throws us. God wasn't absent or uninvolved, but He was silent, at least with Job. It's the mysterious sense of God's silence, which played out in Job's life as God's absence, that makes all of us shake our heads, wondering why.

It must have been like swimming in a vast lake and getting three or four hundred yards offshore when suddenly a freak fog rolls in and surrounds you. You're trapped in this tiny circle of diffused light, but you can't see beyond your arm's reach. You begin to swim toward the shore; at least you think it's the shore, but you're not sure. Then you panic, and you turn and swim in another direction. By now, you've totally lost your orientation. You don't know where the shore is. Your heart rate increases and you decide to float to conserve your strength. Finally, even the eerie light fades, and you know the sun is going down. It gets dark. You listen with every atom of your being. If only you could hear a voice from shore. Muffled, faint, at least it would give you a sense of direction—something to swim toward.

That sense of lostness must have swept over Job as he sat in the rubble of what was once a beautiful and prosperous landscape. His livelihood was gone, ruined. The fresh graves of his children lay before him on a barren, windswept hill. He had lost everything, even his health. He sat in the ashes of his life—crushed, alone, without direction. He could not even hear God's voice. And not knowing where, to say nothing of why, he began to voice his distress, words easily criticized by those sitting in a place of comfort, health, and ease.

Afterward Job opened his mouth and cursed the day of his birth.

> And Job said,
> "Let the day perish on which I was born,
> And the night which said, 'A boy is conceived.'"
>
> "Why did I not die at birth,
> Come forth from the womb and expire?"
>
> Job 3:1–3,11

Those are what I would call words from the lake—words in the fog! Those are the words of a man who doesn't know why! He feels completely abandoned. And he is worse than dead, because he is very much alive in his misery.

> "For my groaning comes at the sight of my food,
> And my cries pour out like water.
> For what I fear comes upon me,
> And what I dread befalls me.
> I am not at ease, nor am I quiet,
> And I am not at rest, but turmoil comes."
>
> Job 3:24–26

Don't criticize Job until you've been there. It is the worst kind of existence. Bad enough to have everything gone and to have your body covered with sores from your head to your feet, but to hear no voice from God. . . .

UNDERSTANDING GOD'S TIMING IN OUR DAY

From that moving account of one man's misery, let me take you to a realm that is not nearly so measurable or tangible—the realm of time. Our time versus God's time.

You and I are locked in a tiny space on this foggy lake of life called the present. Because our entire perspective is based on this moment in which we find ourselves, we speak of the present, the past, and the future. If we want to know the hour or minute or second, we merely look at our watch. If we want to know the day or the month, the year or the century, we look at the calendar. Time. Easily marked, carefully measured. It is all very objective: measurable, understandable, and conscious.

God is not like that at all. As a matter of fact, He lives and moves outside the realm of earthly time—beyond the ticking of our clocks—beyond the turning of our calendar.

God has no night. God has no day. God has no month. God has no year. God has no past, present, or future. Theologians call this the *transcendence* of God. He transcends it all.

We see our life in a sequence of frames, moving from one to another, almost like a movie. Not God. He sees all the movie of our life all at once, in a flash, along with millions and billions of others going on simultaneously—past, present, and future. Which makes our little bit of space on the lake seem like a cage called time.

We sing so easily . . .

> In His time, in His time;
> He makes all things beautiful in His time.
> Lord, please show me every day
> As you're teaching me Your way,
> That You do just what You say in Your time.[43]

But immediately we have a problem. With God there is no "day." And He is not locked into our "time." Our problem is that we are looking at life through the wrong end of the telescope. We are finite creatures, so when it comes to the panorama of God's all-seeing mind and God's transcendent perspective, we are left in a fog.

Philip Yancey, in one of his finest volumes, *Disappointment with God*, writes:

> No matter how we rationalize, God will sometimes *seem* unfair from the perspective of a person trapped in time. Only at the end of time, after we have attained God's level of viewing, after every evil has been punished or forgiven, every illness healed, and the entire universe restored—only then will fairness reign. Then we will understand what role is played by evil, and by the Fall, and by natural law, in an "unfair" event like the death of a child. Until then, we will not know, and can only trust in a God who does know.
>
> We remain ignorant of many details, not because God enjoys keeping us in the dark, but because we have not the faculties to absorb so much light. At a single glance God knows what the world is about and how history will end. But we time-bound creatures have only the most primitive manner of understanding: we can let time pass. Not until history has run its course will we understand how "all things work together for good." Faith means believing in advance what will only make sense in reverse.[44]

And that's hard. It's as hard as moving from the chorus "In His time, in His time; He makes all things beautiful in His time" on Sunday to the foggy yet very real world of pain and loss and sudden earthquakes and unexpected floods and premature deaths on Tuesday morning or Wednesday evening or Friday at midnight.

So what do we do? How do we live in the fog without panic? How do we live our lives in this little space, not knowing where the shore is—especially during the times when we do not hear His reassuring voice? To put it simple and straight, we do it by discovering how God works, by having confidence in Him.

DISCOVERING GOD'S WORKING IN ESTHER'S DAY

In our Bibles, the book just before Job is the Book of Esther. And as we are discovering, it's quite a book. As we've said before, it's the only book in the Bible where God isn't named. Neither is prayer, per se. Furthermore, nothing from Esther is quoted in the New Testament. Strange. We'd be tempted to think He's really absent, but that's hardly the case. His prints are all over this wonderful story. We can see the movement of God's hand throughout the lives of Esther and Mordecai. We can see His moving in the heart of King Ahasuerus. We can see Him as He works His own will even through the wicked plots of Haman. How? Why? Because the book is written from the perspective of God's transcendent presence.

Therefore, when we come to chapter 3 and we come across a sustained period of silence during which the king promotes Haman, you and I want to say, "No! Don't do it. You'll be sorry. He's a bad guy. He hates the Jews. He's going to work out a murderous plan. Don't promote him." But Ahasuerus promotes him. An evil game-plan gets underway—and we want God to stop it, but there's no voice from the shore.

The fog thickens as we watch Haman lay the groundwork for exterminating all the Jews in the entire kingdom of Persia. We watch as the official seal of the king is pressed into soft clay and the edict of death goes forth across the land and throughout all the provinces. We think, *Now, God! Stop this wrong!* But there's no voice from the shore.

It must have been like that for the Jews living in Europe when the Nazis emerged. Hitler's henchmen came—they brutalized, they mocked, they killed—and there was no voice from the shore.

Had we lived in that lake of silence, would we have wondered, *Where is God?* Surely, there would have been such questions.

Elie Wiesel, the great prize-winning writer on the Holocaust, tells in his book, *Night,* how he stood, as a child, hearing the terrorizing sounds of death, viewing the horrible sights of death, smelling burning flesh from the oven. Shocked by it all, he heard a man behind him groan: "Where is God? Where is He?"[45]

Yet, even in such periods of silence, God is at work. If you don't know this, and if you don't believe this, and if you don't remember this when He stays silent, you will panic, you will doubt, you will become cynical, resentful, and brimming with bitterness.

Think of it this way: I've heard great sermons on Joseph. I've also listened to great sermons on Moses. But I have never heard a sermon on the 400-plus years—those "silent years"—that separated Joseph from Moses. We move along in history and we come to Hannah. We love Hannah, this woman of God who prayed for a son. And the wonder boy—Samuel—came. We hear great messages on Hannah, great messages on Samuel. But I don't think I've ever heard a message on 1 Samuel 3:1: "And word from the LORD was rare in those days, visions were infrequent." *The Good News Bible* translates it this way: "There were very few messages from the LORD, and visions from him were quite rare."

We think the prophets were the ones who regularly heard God's voice. Not always. Consider the prophet Habakkuk, who watched unjust events occur back to back, one after another, and they didn't stop. Finally, he could take God's silence no longer, so he said to the Lord, "*Why? And while I'm at it, how long?*" What was the problem? Habakkuk was treading water on the lake! The fog had rolled in. "Others can sing, 'In His time, in His time' all they wish, but right now *I'm drowning.*"

Between Malachi and the birth of the Lord Jesus is another 400-year period you have probably never heard a sermon about. I haven't either. Absolute, stark silence. Not even the writing of a verse of Scripture—for four centuries. That's tough to take.

If you want to discover how God works, not only in Esther's day but in our day, keep these two things in mind.

First: *Life is filled with sustained periods of silence. Often.* But those periods of God's silence are just as significant as the times when He speaks. They're far more painful, but they are nevertheless significant. And during those times on that fog-bound lake, you need ears of faith to listen for His voice.

I recall one of my former parishioners, a medical doctor, saying to me one Sunday morning, "We are waiting right now to know if God wants my family and me on a particular mission field." I could tell from the quiet passion in his voice that he wanted to be there. But it was a time of silence, and he didn't know yet exactly when, or even if, he should go. He was in that all-encompassing waiting period. And it's tough.

But remember, God isn't in the business of repeating history. He's writing a new record regularly, even in those times of silence. His surprising sovereignty often takes time to unfold.

Second: *The turning points of life, the significant events, are often subtle.* A sensitive heart is required to detect those changes.

For example, in Esther, chapter 6, we read that the king couldn't sleep. Now when was the last time that made the news? I don't believe I've ever read this line in all the newspapers I've read: "The president couldn't sleep last night." It's subtle even in the biblical record, but as a result, Mordecai's name oozes out of obscurity, which leads to the missing pieces of the puzzle that are critical to God's plan.

In the mystery of God's timing, subtle things occur that the sensitive heart picks up. That's the role wisdom plays in life. Reading life's subtleties is what Christian maturity is all about. And rather than thrashing around, thinking, *I will not make it through this. I will* never *hear God's voice*, we determine, in wisdom, to watch for the slightest turning of events.

Right after this sleepless night, who's in the court of the king? Of all people, *Haman!* Haman, who still has splinters in his hands from building the gallows on which to hang Mordecai. He showed up early, thinking he, the "fair-haired boy" will get his way. Wrong! The king calls him in and says, "How should we honor someone?" Haman thinks, *Who better to honor than me?* Wrong again! That's not God's plan. He's going to honor *Mordecai.* And Haman ends up eating a huge slice of humble pie, being the one who leads Mordecai through Susa, proclaiming his greatness. I'd call that a rather significant change of events.

It is easy to live like a dullard. Many folks do. It is easy to anticipate that this year will be very much like last and the one before it, when, in fact, chances are good it will be altogether different. So when events begin to turn, realize that none of it is merely coincidental. Remember that. Take the word "coincidental" out of your vocabulary, along with "luck." You can trash them both! You don't need them anymore. *Nothing* is coincidental! "Luck" has no place in a Christian's vocabulary.

In His time and only in His time, He begins to move in subtle ways until, suddenly, as His surprising sovereignty unfolds, a change occurs. Don't fight it. It's God's way of lifting the fog, which always happens when He pleases!

For example, this epochal moment in Esther's life.

> Now the king and Haman came to drink wine with Esther the queen. And the king said to Esther on the second day also as they drank their wine at the banquet, "What is your petition, Queen Esther? It shall be granted you. And what is your request? Even to half the kingdom it shall be done."
>
> Esther 7:1–2

This second banquet is the event—the moment—that breaks the silence. Once again, it's just the three of them: the king, the queen, and the prime minister.

"What is your petition?" the king asks Esther. "What is your request?"

He's already asked that two other times: when she first approached him and he held out his scepter, and then at the first banquet, but Esther never answered him, because the time wasn't right. Esther had a sensitive ear, a wise heart; she sensed something wasn't quite right. So, she didn't push it. She knew when to act—and she knew when to wait.

Are you as sensitive as that? Do you know when to listen? Do you know when to speak up—and when to keep quiet? Do you know how much to say as well as when to say it? Do you have the wisdom to hold back until the right moment? Those things make a difference, you know. Obviously, nobody bats a thousand on matters such as this, but the question is: Are you sufficiently in tune with God to read His subtle signals? It's easy to jump at the first sighting of the fog's lifting.

Esther, though trapped in that fog-bound silence, that little space of limited sight, had not told all that she had on her heart. The time was not right. She sensed that. Until this moment, she hadn't even told the king that she was Jewish. But now the right moment had arrived to break the silence.

As Solomon once wrote, ". . . there is a time for every event under heaven. . . . a time to be silent, and a time to speak" (Eccl. 3:1, 7). Silence was once appropriate, but no longer. One wonders if Esther's heart was beating in her throat as she realized her nation's future hung in the balance of the next few words she would speak and the response of her husband, the king. Once King Ahasuerus opened the door this third time, "Esther then took courage to express her petition."[46]

> Then Queen Esther answered and said, "If I have found favor in your sight, O king, and if it please the king, let my life be given me as my petition, and my people as my request; for we have been sold, I and my people, to be destroyed, to be killed and to be annihilated. Now if we had only been sold as slaves, men and women, I would have remained silent, for the trouble would not be commensurate with the annoyance to the king."
>
> Esther 7:3–4

Talk about the power of a woman! Can you believe Esther's diplomacy and sensitivity, even in the midst of pleading for her life and the lives of her people? "If we were only being sold into slavery, I wouldn't have troubled you with this matter. You have so many important matters to worry about, I wouldn't have bothered you. But he wants to annihilate us!" Esther beautifully portrays in this moment the character qualities of greatness. Her husband is all ears!

> Then King Ahasuerus asked Queen Esther, "Who is he, and where is he, who would presume to do thus?"
>
> Esther 7:5

At this point, I confess that my response might have been something like, "What do you mean, *who is he*? You were there when Haman proposed this heinous thing. You gave him your seal to sign the edict. What do you mean, 'who is he?' Open your eyes!" Thankfully, I wasn't there to blow it.

We live in a world of preoccupied people. They too live in a fog. Who knows how many edicts Ahasuerus signed that day? Who knows how many pressing matters of government were on his mind? The king had countless decisions to make. And Haman, who was a trusted official, had proposed it in such a way that he seemed to be solving a problem that directly affected the good of the kingdom. So the king probably signed it without giving it a great deal of attention, believing that Haman, a man he trusted, knew what he was doing.

Suddenly, however, things had changed. Don't ever try to convince me that some situation in this life is absolutely permanent. God can move in the heart of a king. He can move an entire nation. He can bring down the once-impenetrable Iron Curtain. He can change the mind of your stubborn mate. He can move in the affairs of your community. He can alter decisions of presidents and prime ministers and present-day kings and national dictators. No barrier is too high, no chasm is too wide for Him, because He is not limited by space or time, by the visible or the invisible. Remember, He lives in a realm that transcends all that. He is all-powerful. And when God is ready to move, He moves. And when He does, hang on. You're in for the ride of your life.

Realizing that her moment had arrived, Esther neither stammered nor hesitated.

> And Esther said, "A foe and an enemy is this wicked Haman!" Then Haman became terrified before the king and queen.
>
> Esther 7:6

So Esther, clothed in strength and dignity, answers with the same kind of courage she has displayed since her decision to risk all: "Who is responsible? That man. Our enemy, that wicked Haman!"

> As Esther has put the case Haman is a traitor to the king as well as an enemy of the Jews. As she points to this wicked Haman she senses her triumph and notes the terror of Haman. He might well be terrified. Esther's words to the king had been an eye-opener for him also, because

he had not known Esther's nationality. The realization that he had in-advertently threatened the queen's life was a knock-out blow on top of his earlier humiliation.[47]

Now old Haman hasn't had the best of days. The past twenty-four to thirty-six hours have brought him nothing but grief. First he had to trumpet the praises of Mordecai throughout the city of Susa, and now the queen herself is accusing him to the king. He is downright *terrified*, and rightly so.

We, on the other hand, are cheering. Because we want *justice!* We want good rewarded, and we want evil punished. Haman ought not to be running loose calling the shots. They ought to finish him off. Which is exactly what the king does.

> Then Harbonah, one of the eunuchs who were before the king said, "Behold indeed, the gallows standing at Haman's house fifty cubits high, which Haman made for Mordecai who spoke good on behalf of the king!" And the king said, "Hang him on it."
> So they hanged Haman on the gallows which he had prepared for Mordecai, and the king's anger subsided.
>
> Esther 7:9–10

All the time Haman was having the gallows built, he could see—enthusiastically anticipate—Mordecai impaled there. Now, he is condemned to die there himself. We call this irony. Theologians call it sovereignty. I call it God's *surprising* sovereignty!

I can remember a time early on in my ministerial training, when the sovereignty of God was frightening to me. Not understanding its implications as fully as I do now some thirty-five years later, I felt it would make me passive and virtually irresponsible. Furthermore, I feared what it would do to my theology of evangelism. If I really threw myself into this doctrine, God could become a distant deity, sort of a celestial brute, pushing and maneuvering His way through nameless humanity, as He did what He pleased to get what He wanted. I could see my zeal waning and my passion for souls drained to the point of indifference.

Through a series of events far too numerous and complicated to describe, I've come to realize that, rather than being frightened by God's sovereignty, I'm comforted in it. Since He alone is God, and since He, being God, "does all things well" and in doing them has only "good" as His goal, how could I do anything but embrace it?

Does that mean I can explain it? No, only rarely, when hindsight yields insight. Does that mean I always anticipate it? No, like you, I occasionally rush to judgment or respond in panic, wondering why He is so silent, allowing wrong to run its course so long. But looking back in more reasonable moments, with my emotions under better control (*His* control!), I can see what He was about. I can even see why He delayed, or why He acted when He did. Usually, I freely admit, I think He is awfully slow (I can't number the times I've pleaded, "O, God—please *hurry up!*") and I am usually surprised, though I shouldn't be, at how beautifully things work out.

But, the good news is that I've come full circle. I find enormous comfort in knowing, in the final analysis, God is God and He will have His way when He pleases and for His glory. What could be better than that? In all the mystery of His waiting and working and in all the wrong of our doing and undoing, He can still be trusted. The big thing is that you and I remain sensitive to those moments when He breaks the silence (which we're tempted to call absence) and suddenly intervenes on our behalf. Furthermore, I'm more than ever concerned over the lost! But in the final analysis, their salvation rests with Him, not with me.

Esther's ability to cooperate at those all-important moments causes her to stand head and shoulders above her contemporaries.

BEING SENSITIVE TO GOD'S INTERVENTIONS EVERY DAY

Since we are trapped in this earthbound cage, this little space where light is often diffused and God is sometimes silent, how can we be sensitive to His interventions? What do we do when we, like Job, struggle in the fog with God's silence, when we're convinced that His silence means absence?

Please, be assured, He is not absent. He may be silent, but He's not absent. So let me close this chapter with three "life preservers" that have helped me stay afloat during my own scary experiences on the lake, when the fog seemed unusually thick.

First: *The fog on your lake is neither accidental nor fatal.* So while swimming, listen very carefully and patiently for His voice. Some days you will be seized with panic and dog-paddle like mad. You'll try various approaches: breaststroke, butterfly, backstroke, float. But all the time, you want to be listening for His voice. I urge you to listen with great sensitivity, because His message will come in various ways.

I get nervous around some people and the way they talk about hearing God or seeing Him at work. Sometimes I freely admit that I want to recommend a good therapist. Especially when I hear people say things like, "The Lord spoke to me in my kitchen at 2:15 this morning." Or, "God found me a parking space today." I consider these folks "bumper-sticker Christians." They're often scary folks, almost spooky. Miracles are everyday occurrences to them. They see skywriting in the clouds, and they hear voices in the night. Hear me well, that's not the kind of "voice" I'm talking about.

God gave you a mind. God gave you reason. God gave you a unique sensitivity; it's built into your spiritual system, and each person's system is tuned differently. God wants to reveal His will to you and to teach you while you are waiting. So while you are waiting, don't start searching for spooky stuff. We walk by faith, not by sight (2 Cor. 5:7). Get into His Word. Get on your knees. Accept counsel from those who are maturing and balanced believers, solidly biblical in their theology and in their own life. And wait. Wait! Don't try to read the stars, and while you're at it, stay away from people who tell you they can. The answers are not on your palms or in some astrology column or in the flash of a crystal. However, there are tangible things to connect with. Passages of Scripture that bring comfort and insight. Messages that enlighten and enliven. Certain people you respect. Tap into those, wait, and listen with a sensitive ear. Like Esther, don't rush into big decisions. And may I be painfully direct? Don't talk so much! Believers who are maturing not only respect God's silence, they model it as well.

Second: *The workings of God are not related to our clocks; they are related to our crises.* That's why God doesn't care if this is the last day you can buy that car on sale. It doesn't bother God that it is the first day of summer or high noon or a quarter after seven or ten minutes to one in the morning. His timing is unrelated to Planet Earth's clock time. So while waiting, look beyond the present.

The best way to do that is to *pray!* Make your life a life of prayer. Tell Him, in anguish if necessary, the horror of the waiting. Express your panic. Tell Him you're trapped. (Ask Him to hurry up, if that helps. He can handle it!). You don't know how you can stay afloat much longer. In those moments, ask Him to help you see beyond the pain of the present.

Prayer supports me when I can't quite grasp the meaning of something I'm struggling with, like when I'm dealing with big decisions or working with difficult people. Prayer gives me a calming perspective.

Third: *The surprises in store are not merely ironic or coincidental, they are sovereignly designed.* While anticipating, trust Him for justice. You may not live to see that justice, but it will come. He is a just God; you know He is. So trust Him for it.

I have found, while in the fog, that my great temptation is either to doubt or to deny—maybe they're the same thing—to doubt or to deny that He is even at work. But, more often than not, when something looks like it's the absolute *end,* it is really the *beginning.* I can see this later, when I look back.

Think of the cross. The Roman officials applauded. The Jewish officials rejoiced. "Finally, we got rid of him, that troublemaker! We're glad that's over." Yet three days later, He was alive again. What seemed like an ending was only the beginning.

Esther, our heroine, is a lovely model to follow. And her story is certainly one to remember. But the best focus of all? God Himself. How perfectly He works, how sovereignly He controls, and how remarkably He changes the face of things, once He moves in. A queen who was once passive is suddenly in charge. A king who was once duped is now informed. An enemy who was only moments away from exterminating a nation is now an object of scorn. And even those ghastly gallows, once built for a Jew named Mordecai, will soon pierce the body of a Gentile named Haman.

When will we ever learn? At the precise moment when it will have its greatest impact, God ceases His silence and sovereignly makes His moves. And when He does, it's full of surprises.

CHAPTER NINE

And the Walls Came Tumbling Down

We are examining the life of a woman named Esther. She lived multiple centuries ago, surrounded by people we've never known in a culture we've never seen, and yet so many of her experiences are as relevant and real as yesterday's events or this morning's newscast. In my opinion, that is one of the most exciting reasons for studying the Bible.

Names and places, cultures and methods continue to change, but the underlying principles that were at work back then remain just as true today. And the building materials from which life's foundations are formed are equally timeless. Universal sinfulness, that works itself out in powerful ways like deceitful schemes and treacherous acts, is no different now than when Haman set out to destroy the Jews in ancient Persia. Thankfully, there is an even more-powerful force that stands against such wickedness—divine righteousness, that opposes, restrains, and blocks the evil plans arranged by evil people. In our present study those righteous acts are carried out by people like Mordecai and Esther. Down through time those names change and their heroic deeds differ, but the effect remains the same. Right ultimately prevails over wrong. It did in Esther's day, and it will in ours.

But there are often long periods of time where the light of hope gets so dim, we're tempted to question that fact. Walls of wrong can be built so high and thick, we wonder if they will stand forever. But this is where history helps. Looking back, we rediscover hope because we find recorded evidence that no wall, no matter how imposing it may have seemed in its day, continues to stand.

ALL WALLS FINALLY FALL

All walls fall . . . eventually. No matter how well-constructed or long-standing it is, the wall will fall. It may be as intimidating as an angry giant or as silent as thin air and just as invisible, like the stubborn will of a person or the bitter spirit of an individual. But all walls finally fall.

Anyone who knows even a little history knows how true that is. To this day, archaeologists' spades continue to unearth the fallen walls of the world's great empires. Egyptian walls. Grecian walls. Roman walls. French walls. German walls. Russian walls.

I look into the Scriptures and I see similar situations. And I find myself asking, *Why do we even have walls in the first place?* I love the moving words of poet Robert Frost, "Before I built a wall, I'd ask to know what I was walling in or walling out." And so should we.

The Egyptians should have asked what they were walling in and what they were walling out. But they didn't, so for 430 years the Hebrews lived in abject slavery until God sent Moses to Pharaoh. Then, by the power of the living God, that long-standing, seemingly impenetrable wall came tumbling down.

A few years later, Joshua and the Hebrews invaded the Promised Land near the walled city of Jericho. To the naked eye that was one imposing structure of stone. But it was as *nothing* in the presence of the living God. Three words tell it all: "The wall collapsed" (Josh. 6:20 NIV).

Jerusalem's walls looked so formidable, so strong. The city flew its own flag under numerous kings. But Nebuchadnezzar broke down those walls.

Subsequently, the walls of the Babylonian kingdom were conquered during the reign of Belshazzar. The great Medo-Persian empire emerged and appeared unconquerable until Alexander the Great swept across the scene. The world certainly must have thought the Greeks were in power forever—but then came the Romans with their Caesars.

The Romans believed their walls would stand forever. They were strong, no doubt about it, but they ultimately fell beneath the invasion of other barbarian hordes more ruthless and powerful than they!

All walls finally fall. Even our own. Even those walls built up against us. In the final analysis, Christ conquers! As Paul wrote, "He himself is our peace . . . and has destroyed the barrier, the dividing wall of hostility . . . " (Eph. 2:14, NIV). In the words of Betsie ten Boom, ". . . there is no pit so deep but that He is not deeper still."[48] Let me suggest a paraphrase that ties in with my point here: "There is no wall so great but that He is not greater still."

WALLS THAT FELL IN ESTHER'S DAY

All this brings us to the little slice of history found in the eighth chapter of the Book of Esther. By now you're probably asking yourself what all of this has to do with Esther? Everything, really. This is a chapter where a heart is so hard that it seemed it would never change . . . but it changes. The wall of a stubborn human heart collapses. Prior to this chapter, the scene was dark, but here God floods it with light.

To borrow again from Betsie's words: there is no heart so hard that He cannot change it. There is no writing so permanent that He cannot erase it. There is no scene so dark that He cannot brighten it.

An Unchangeable Heart

> On that day King Ahasuerus gave the house of Haman, the enemy of the Jews, to Queen Esther; and Mordecai came before the king, for Esther had disclosed what he was to her.
>
> Esther 8:1

Can this really be? Remember the mighty King Ahasuerus? The story begins with him, front and center. When the curtain first went up, he was the main character. Let me remind you.

Now it took place in the days of Ahasuerus, the Ahasuerus who reigned from India to Ethiopia over 127 provinces, in those days as King Ahasuerus sat on his royal throne which was in Susa the capital . . .

Esther 1:1–2

This man is powerful. This man can, with just a wave of his hand, cause people to live or die. This is the man who got rid of his wife, Queen Vashti, simply because she displeased him. This is the man who decided to promote Haman, who hated the Jews, to the position of prime minister. This is the man who said to Haman, "Here is my ring." Another way of saying, "Take my credit card. You sign for me. You pass the edicts." And those edicts were permanent! This is the man who willingly assented to Haman's plan to rid the kingdom of Persia of an entire race of people. When this king's thumb went up, people lived. When it turned down, they were history.

And all of a sudden, this is the man who changes his mind.

He has held out his golden scepter to Esther and said, "Why are you troubled? What can I do for you? I would give up to half my kingdom for you." He has listened to Esther's plea, and, as a result, has ordered Haman, his own recently appointed prime minister, to be impaled on the gallows upon which Haman had hoped to hang Mordecai. Now, he has given Haman's entire estate to Esther.

There is evidence in extra-biblical literature, and I'm thinking particularly of the Greek historian Herodotus, that the property of condemned criminals reverted back to the crown. So in this case, the estate of Haman, a condemned criminal, would normally become the property of the king. But of all things, the king doesn't keep it. Instead, he gives it to Esther, who in turn gives it to Mordecai, for she now tells the king about Mordecai's relationship to her.

And the king took off his signet ring which he had taken away from Haman, and gave it to Mordecai. And Esther set Mordecai over the house of Haman.

Then Esther spoke again to the king, fell at his feet, wept, and implored him to avert the evil scheme of Haman the Agagite and his plot which he had devised against the Jews.

Esther 8:2–3

No heart is so stubborn that God cannot penetrate it. No will is so determined that He cannot break through it, whenever He so desires. No one—no matter who and no matter how powerful—is a match for the living God. A repeating of Solomon's counsel is timely here:

> The king's heart is like channels of water in the hand of the LORD;
> He turns it wherever He wishes.
> Every man's way is right in his own eyes,
> But the LORD weighs the hearts.

Proverbs 21:1–2

The king's heart is like mush, like soft putty, we could say like play dough, in the hands of the Lord.

Just for a moment imagine another name in that proverb in place of "the king." Someone who is giving you grief perhaps. It may be one of your own grown, wayward children. Maybe it's someone who represents a formidable presence. Someone who haunts you and maybe wishes to bring you down. Stubborn person, right? Strong-hearted individual, correct? Imagine that heart that is so hard, so granitelike, changing into soft putty in the hands of the Lord. It's possible! There is no heart so stubborn that it cannot become breakable in the hands of the Lord.

Many years ago, in another place and at another time in my life, I went through a dreadful experience with a person who decided to make me his enemy. I still do not know why. It remains a mystery. Nevertheless, it occurred. This individual decided to make my life miserable. He watched my every move. He questioned my decisions. He cast doubts on my ministry. This person applied pressure, sometimes to the point where I thought I would scream. I don't know how much he said to others. I never asked. But he said enough to me and was bullying and intimidating enough that I became frightened, especially when I realized he carried a gun. Eventually, on one occasion, he threatened me with it.

One bitterly cold Sunday after church I went home and fell across our bed, not even taking off my overcoat. I cried out to the Lord. I wept audibly until I could not cry another tear. I had come to my wit's end. I was exhausted, trying everything I knew to do to bring about a change. *Nothing* changed! This man had a heart like King Ahasuerus.

I'll share with you later in this chapter how things changed. But the point I am making here is that you may have some such individual who has one major goal in life: to make your life miserable. You may work alongside him, or you may go to school with him or even room with him. You may be married to him, or have once been married to him.

Now then, it is essential that in the midst of this to remember there is no wall so strong that Almighty God is not stronger still. There is no will so stubborn that He is not able to soften it. If God can change the heart of an Ahasuerus, He can change *any* heart—*any heart!* Read that again. You who live your days intimidated and threatened, anxious over the falling of the next shoe, listen to this counsel! God is able to take the heart of anyone and change it, just as He did with the heart of this king. Yes, *anyone.*

An Irrevocable Edict

> Then Esther spoke again to the king, fell at his feet, wept, and implored him to avert the evil scheme of Haman the Agagite and his plot which he had devised against the Jews.
>
> Esther 8:3

Haman may be gone, but his edict is still in place. That was the trouble with those Medo-Persia edicts. Once they were passed, they couldn't be rescinded. Listen to Daniel 6, where three times we read similar words:

> "Now, O king, establish the injunction and sign the document so that it may not be changed, according to the law of the Medes and Persians, which may not be revoked."

. . . "The statement is true, according to the law of the Medes and Persians, which may not be revoked."

Then these men came by agreement to the king and said to the king, "Recognize, O king, that it is a law of the Medes and Persians that no injunction or statute which the king establishes may be changed."

Daniel 6:8,12,15

Haman may be dead, but the edict is still very much alive. It has been written, *it will be done!* It is irrevocable. The Jews will die in December. Knowing this, Esther weeps. If I may say so, there are times when the genuine, compassionate tears of a woman are absolutely irresistible. Rare is the man who can be near them and not be softened by them. A woman's tears can melt the hardest heart!

Consider Ahasuerus, the mighty king! At this point, he extends the golden scepter to her, which is his way of saying, "Speak. I'm listening."

Then she said, "If it pleases the king and if I have found favor before him and the matter seems proper to the king and I am pleasing in his sight, let it be written to revoke the letters devised by Haman, the son of Hammedatha the Agagite, which he wrote to destroy the Jews who are in all the king's provinces.

Esther 8:5

Let it be written? But it is already written. Yet she is pleading for the king to revoke what has been written. We who live in a culture where such things occur with a measure of regularity, hardly raise an eyebrow when someone in authority changes his or her mind. But back then, it was something unheard of in the land of Persia.

"For how can I endure to see the calamity which shall befall my people, and how can I endure to see the destruction of my kindred?"

Esther 8:6

Certainly this is the kind of situation which makes you wonder if there is a wall so thick that God cannot penetrate it.

> So King Ahasuerus said to Queen Esther and to Mordecai the Jew, "Behold, I have given the house of Haman to Esther, and him they have hanged on the gallows because he had stretched out his hands against the Jews. Now you write to the Jews as you see fit, in the king's name, and seal it with the king's signet ring; for a decree which is written in the name of the king and sealed with the king's signet ring may not be revoked."
>
> Esther 8:7–8

"Here's the pen," says the king. "You write *another* edict—this one overriding the other." Isn't that incredible?

Do you think it isn't worthwhile to stand against wrong laws? Do you think it is futile to stand in favor of life in the womb and against abortion? Here is a classic example of why we should boldly stand and fight to affirm truth, even though it appears existing laws will never change.

> So the king's scribes were called at that time in the third month (that is, the month Sivan), on the twenty-third day; and it was written according to all that Mordecai commanded to the Jews, the satraps, the governors, and the princes of the provinces which extended from India to Ethiopia, 127 provinces, to every province according to its script, and to every people according to their language, as well as to the Jews according to their script and their language. And he wrote in the name of King Ahasuerus, and sealed it with the king's signet ring, and sent letters by couriers on horses, riding on steeds sired by the royal stud.
>
> Esther 8:9–10

So the message goes out, with the authority of the king, and carried by couriers riding the finest horses in the kingdom.

In them the king granted the Jews who were in each and every city the right to assemble and to defend their lives, to destroy, to kill, and to annihilate the entire army of any people or province which might attack them, including children and women, and to plunder their spoil, on one day in all the provinces of King Ahasuerus, the thirteenth day of the twelfth month (that is, the month Adar). A copy of the edict to be issued as law in each and every province, was published to all the peoples, so that the Jews should be ready for this day to avenge themselves on their enemies.

Esther 8:11–13

No, the law of the Medes and Persians couldn't be changed. The law Haman had written had to stay on the books. But because the heart of the king had been softened by the pleas of Esther, he provided a way by which that law might never come into affect—or would at least be neutralized. The Jews could protect themselves. In fact, they could do more than that. They could take the lives of anyone who might attack them, including women and children, and they had a right to plunder and take ownership of their possessions. So at least it was an even playing field. The Jews now had their own defense, established of all things, by the Persian law.

The couriers, hastened and impelled by the king's command, went out, riding on the royal steeds; and the decree was given out in Susa the capital.

Esther 8:14

The decree Mordecai wrote was sent out in the third month . . . Sivan (June-July) 474. Since this was a little over two months after Haman's decree (3:12) the Jews had about nine months to prepare themselves for conflict. . . . As was the case with the previous decree (cf. 3:12), this one too was dispatched . . . by horsemen throughout the whole empire from India to Cush . . . and was written in the appropriate languages for each province. The edict gave the Jews . . . the right to protect themselves and the right to annihilate (cf. 3:13; 7:4) and plunder any group that fought against them. The Jews could take away the property of their enemies as Mordecai had "taken away" the property of Haman.[49]

Amazing! And to think these rights provided for all the Jews were granted by the same man who earlier had virtually sealed their doom.

You may not simply have some person after you. You may have some document, something that's been written that seems irrevocable—some magazine article, some newspaper article, some transcript, some occupational report, some lawsuit, whatever. Because it's in writing, it looks so intimidating, so unerasable, so legal. And you're reading these words, thinking, *Yeah, but if you only knew who's behind that.* That's my whole point here! Who is *anybody* compared to the living Lord? I don't care who's behind that document. We serve a sovereign God who has yet to go "Ahh!" when He finds anything on this earth. Nothing frightens Him. Nothing causes Him to do a neck jerk. He's in charge! We live "in the shelter of the Most High." We "abide in the shadow of the Almighty" (Ps. 91:1). Nothing is to hard for Him!

> "And all the inhabitants of the earth are accounted as nothing,
> But He does according to His will in the host of heaven
> And among the inhabitants of earth;
> And no one can ward off His hand
> Or say to Him, 'What hast thou done?'"
>
> Daniel 4:35

He's the God you and I serve, child of God. He's the Lord we worship, my friend. He's the One who is your refuge and fortress.

When God steps in to rewrite the record, the results are amazing. Not only will every knee bow before Him ultimately, but every lie will be exposed, every falsehood forever overturned. Do not fear what your enemies may write about or against you. It is not eternal. Someday the final books will be opened and the only true record will be read. Talk about neck jerks!

An Impenetrable Gloom

A gloom had settled over the city of Susa and the other provinces of the kingdom. The scene probably resembled the atmosphere at Auschwitz or Dachau or Birkenau. No one laughed. Every day brought everyone another twenty-four hours closer to doom. But look . . . look closely:

> Then Mordecai went out from the presence of the king in royal robes of blue and white, with a large crown of gold and a garment of fine linen and purple; and the city of Susa shouted and rejoiced. For the Jews there was light and gladness and joy and honor. And in each and every province, and in each and every city, wherever the king's commandment and his decree arrived, there was gladness and joy for the Jews, a feast and a holiday. And many among the peoples of the land became Jews, for the dread of the Jews had fallen on them.
>
> Esther 8:15–17

It was like Thanksgiving and Christmas and New Year's all rolled into one. It was like Berlin on the ninth of November, 1989! It was like nothing they had ever seen before. They would sing all night and all the next day because the gloom was lifted! The darkness wasn't impenetrable after all. It just seemed so.

Do you live in a place of gloom and darkness, where laughter does not echo off the walls? Has your life become grim or even borderline tragic? While others go home to the love and warmth of a family, do you go home alone to the awful memory of broken relationships, remorse, and guilt? Perhaps your last sounds of the day are the clanging of a cell door and some guard yelling, "Lights out!" Do you look with longing at a scene like this one in Esther?

As I wrote at the beginning of this chapter, Esther's story is no irrelevant slice of history tucked away in the folds of an ancient scroll. These principles are still at work today. This is life, as relevant today as when it was first recorded. This is written to people who face intimidating, stubborn souls. Perhaps they live with them, are married to them, or have grown children like that. This is written to people whose lives have been scarred by documents and lawsuits, bad reports, or rumors. This is written to people whose lives are lived within the thick, stone walls of depression and doom. And this chapter announces in bold letters: *There is hope!*

WALLS THAT FALL ON ANY DAY

Walls fall every day. But we cannot predict when yours will be falling.

There is a Christian college in the Midwest where there was once a large lovely tree that was a central part of the landscape. It was one of the places students chose to meet and talk. For decades this giant oak brought beauty to the campus and shade to thousands of students. Then one day, a loud crack echoed across the campus as this leafy monument of memories plunged to the ground. When they examined it, they noticed that disease had been growing within this massive tree, to the point where all that was left was the outer trunk; inside, was nothing more than an empty shell. So, when the harsh wind blew that day, the hollow tree fell. And so it is in our lives.

Remember the man I mentioned earlier, who years ago made my life such a misery? Well, this man had a change of heart. He moved to another, much smaller town. He and his family wanted to find a church; in fact, he wanted to *start* a church. One problem: he couldn't find anyone to preach, so he decided to start with several sets of tapes. And guess whose tapes he decided to use? *Mine.* I would never have guessed that would happen had I lived a thousand years. But the mighty hand of God changed him. He who had been so tough and stubborn was softened by the Lord through several painful blows, or so I was told. And finally, brought to a state of need and dependence, he turned back to the very things he had earlier resisted.

God is in the business of breaking down walls. The wall may be *your own stubborn will.* You may be one of those individuals who has determined, "This is the way I will go, and I will get there, regardless. No one will stand in my way."

When I was a student at seminary, back in the fall of 1959, I heard a speaker conclude his message with a statement that has stayed with me all these years. He said, "When God wants to do an impossible task, he takes an impossible person and crushes him."

A. W. Tozer says much the same thing in one of his works: "It's doubtful whether God can bless a man greatly until He has hurt him deeply."[50] I've quoted that and received mail from people who have said, "You make God appear awfully cruel." It's not cruelty, it's sovereignty. Your stubborn will does not intimidate Him. Painful though it will be for you, He *will* bring you to your knees.

Some of you are children of God. But the way you live your life, very few can tell it, because you are so stubborn! You will *not* give in! But I say to you, you are no match for God. He will break you. He will bend you. He may even have to crush you, because He wants your heart.

The wall may be *a damaging document*. Such walls fall every day. It's amazing how the truth emerges. That which appeared so permanent suddenly gives way in the light of truth. The problem is, in the waiting period it is dreadful for the person hanging in the balance.

Take hope. Take heart. This will pass. The truth will become known.

Every day, *walls of depression and gloom* are penetrated by the wonderful presence of the living God.

> Weeping may last for the night,
> But a shout of joy comes in the morning.
>
> Psalm 30:5

Hurting people gain a perspective that those who have not yet been hurt lack. I often turn back to the words of David:

> Before I was afflicted, I went astray,
> But now I keep Thy word.

> It is good for me that I was afflicted,
> That I may learn Thy statutes.

I know, O LORD, that Thy judgments are righteous,
And that in faithfulness Thou hast afflicted me.

Psalm 119:67,71,75

"How can I put this to work?" you ask. "How can I make this happen? I want this."

Let me answer specifically. What you need is both the presence of the Savior and the perspective of the cross alive and at work in your life. His cross casts its shadow across all of life, and it makes it bearable. You need the Lord God living in your life, operating in masterful control. You need Him there to prompt perspective and to give endurance, or you will fade in anxiety, and your enemy will win the day. A stubborn will will disturb your peace. A document that's damaging will destroy you. The gloom that comes will depress you. If you're like many, you will turn to a bottle or some drug to get you through. You'll opt to fill up the hollow loneliness with a lifestyle that you will later regret. How much better to turn it all over to Him who has the power you need, and to trust Him to change a will you cannot dodge—including yours!

Esther's story may be ancient, but it lives on, doesn't it? And how beautifully the Lord steps in to make things right, just when He was needed the most. He's never late, but He does seem to delay His involvement longer than we would prefer.

Can you imagine Esther's relief, following her husband's new edict? And while you're imagining, can you picture the gladness and joy all across the city of Susa—in fact, "in each and every province and in each and every city"—once the news started spreading? We're talking one massive party, in-the-street celebration for all the Jews, singing and music and dancing and laughter and wall-to-wall joy! (My kind of place!) When those old walls of stubbornness and fear and gloom are torn down, what's better to do than celebrate? They "let it all out," we'd say.

And talk about becoming infectious! The last verse of this chapter concludes with a curious statement: "And many among the peoples of the land became Jews. . . ." The gladness of their hearts, the joy on their faces, the delight in their dancing, the overall, unrestrained fun among them attracted others to their Lord. It always will. People cannot stay away from the audacious joy of God's people!

My mentor and later my colleague in ministry for so many years, the late Ray Stedman, expresses this much better than I:

> When, because of your faith, your life too becomes perceptibly different; when your reactions are quite opposite to what the situation seems to call for and your activities can no longer be explained in terms of your personality; that is when your neighborhood will sit up and take notice. In the eyes of the world, it is not our relationship with Jesus Christ that counts; it is our resemblance to him! In the midst of circumstances that look like certain defeat, there is no more powerful testimony than the joy produced by faith.[51]

And so . . . the scene had changed in every way as Esther returned to her palace room that evening. She had done what needed to be done. She had ignored protocol and interrupted the king. She had waited until the time was best to say what she had to say. She boldly stood against wickedness and courageously exposed Haman's cruel plan. She then pled for her people, whom God preserved through the new edict of the king. She did what was right, and as she lay down that night, exhausted, she could hear the music and laughter from the Jews in the streets of Susa. She thanked her God for bringing down all those walls that no one but He could have handled, for opening doors no one but He could have opened, for preserving lives no one but He could have preserved. How reassuring was the joy of those Jews!

> And the night shall be filled with music,
> And the cares that infest the day,
> Shall fold their tents like the Arabs,
> And as silently steal away.
>
> —Henry Wadsworth Longfellow

With a happy and grateful heart deep within her, with all the cares of the day finally behind her, Esther listened to her people as they celebrated. She smiled in the night and fell fast asleep.

Chapter Ten

The Limitations of Retaliation

Let's start this chapter with several questions:

- Have you ever lost your temper?
- Have you ever been so busy that your prayers got squeezed out of your priorities?
- Ever worried so much that you felt sick inside?
- Ever eaten too much so that you put on weight?
- Ever found thoughts of envy and anger and materialism and lust coming back, even though you told the Lord, "This is going to be the last time I'll have to come to You with this problem?"
- Ever said too much and then had to go back and try to make it right, even apologize, only to say too much again a little later on?
- Ever driven faster than the speed limit?

THE TEMPTATION TO GO TOO FAR

All of these things could fall under the category of yielding to the temptation to go too far. And there isn't a person who can honestly answer those questions any other way but yes. In fact, YES! Every one of us has gotten angry and lost our tempers, only to regret it. Every one of us has allowed our schedules to get so overloaded that, looking back over the week, we must admit to ourselves, if we're honest, we've not stopped to pray even once. Every one of us has eaten too much, even when we swore we wouldn't. (If we drank like we ate, every one of us would be an alcoholic.) Who hasn't fought and fought and fought yet again the old battle with lust or greed or materialism or anger or envy? Every one of us has said more than we should have, more often than not. Even though we apologize, we do it again and again and again. And who hasn't pushed the pedal to the metal? I could go on and on. Some go too far in their fitness fad—too far, too much, too often, too extreme. Some go too far spending money—out of control, getting into debt. Some go too far with perfectionism, too far with work—we've even coined the word "workaholic" because of it. The list of familiar sins is virtually endless.

This syndrome is described beautifully in one verse in the Scriptures, Romans 7:19.

> For the good that I wish, I do not do; but I practice the very evil that
> I do not wish.

The Living Bible renders it,

> When I want to do good, I don't; and when I try not to do wrong, I
> do it anyway.

And Phillips paraphrases it:

> I don't accomplish the good I set out to do, and the evil I don't really
> want to do, I find I'm always doing it.

Every one of us could answer back to Paul, "Amen, that's me. I've been there. I live there." We are an out-of-control people living in an out-of-control society.

I remember reading *The Hundred Yard Lie,* the story of corruption of college football and what we can do to stop it, written by Rick Telander. Rick played football for Northwestern University, made the Big-10, was a draft choice for the Kansas City Chiefs, and was later the lead sports-writer for college ball for *Sport's Illustrated.* Before I was more than seventeen pages into the book, I came across this candid comment:

> I had material all over my office in Chicago, piles of information, books, clippings, quotes, scrawlings, jotted insights of varying per-ceptiveness and naiveté, statistics, brochures, studies, charts, letters and notes that I'd been collecting for years, poems, photos, apho-risms, headlines, even my own college helmet with its cracking leather cheek pads, and a couple of footballs I sometimes just held that com-bined to tell me what I felt. Big-time college football is out of control, rotten from the foundation up.[52]

Even a game, a sport, designed to bring cheer and enthusiasm and healthy competition to a university is, in that man's opinion, *out of control,* corrupt, rotten.

It's like our bodies don't cooperate with our brains. Our minds make great promises that our bodies don't fulfill. Like the pianist who shouted to the soloist, "I'm playing on the white keys and I'm playing on the black keys, so why must you sing in the cracks?" My mind says, "I play on the white keys and the black keys." My body answers back, "I play in the cracks. I live there." The problem, plain and simple, is losing control.

THE KEY TO HOLDING BACK

There is an answer to this daily dilemma, a solution that is easy to identify. There is a secret to holding back. It's also found in the Scriptures in a wonderful list in Galatians 5. It is a lifetime project described in one hyphenated word at the end of the list of the fruit of the Spirit.

But the fruit of the Spirit is love, joy, peace, patience, kindness, goodness, faithfulness, gentleness, self-control; against such things there is no law.

Galatians 5:22–23

"Self-control" . . . that's the key . . . that's the answer. Richard Walters has described self-control as follows.

Self-control is managing our attitudes, feelings, and actions so they serve our long-term best interests and those of others. Self-control comes to people who learn discipline and social skills. It increases in those who accept God's grace in their lives and who seek to know and apply divine truth in a disciplined manner.[53]

The best synonym for self-control is "discipline." Interesting word *self-control*. We use it often but rarely analyze it, even when we come across it in the Bible. Self-control means "inner strength."

This word [self-control] is a compound of . . . two Greek words . . . which literally mean *strength in* or *inner strength and power*. It speaks of one who has power and mastery over his [or her] desires, particularly over sensual appetites.[54]

The fruit of the Spirit is self-control. Self-control frees us from slavery. Self-control stops bad habits. It checks us. It halts us. When it comes to retaliation, self-control restrains us. Without it, we gear up to get even.

Esther's story is a natural for a discussion of retaliation. Webster defines *retaliation* as, "to repay in kind, to return like for like . . . to get revenge." Or, as we more commonly say, "to get even, to get back at someone."

I was just an eleven-year-old boy when the Second World War ended, but I remember learning a lifelong lesson in character from one of my heroes, General Douglas MacArthur. At the end of the war, after the surrender was signed, he requested that President Truman allow him to stay in the land of Japan so he could help bring back the dignity of the Japanese people as he assisted them in putting their country back on its feet after our atomic bombs had leveled the cities of Hiroshima and Nagasaki. Something in the heart of Douglas MacArthur prompted him to step back into that place of devastation and help those who had been our enemies. While many (most?) in America entertained thoughts of revenge, MacArthur was different. "They need a government that works," he suggested. "They need their dignity. They need hope. They need new strength to go on and rebuild."

That's the opposite of retaliation. One without such a spirit would have said, "Grind their faces into the mud! Keep them from *ever* becoming a nation again. They need to pay dearly for what they did to us at Pearl Harbor. Let 'em suffer . . . they deserve it!"

This same spirit was also illustrated beautifully in the life of Corrie ten Boom, who lost her beloved sister Betsie in a Nazi death camp. She could never forget the face of that brutal guard who had made life so miserable for her and for her family. Years later, as she stood to speak of the love and grace of Christ, she looked out and saw that face in the audience. She described the enormity of feelings that floated up into her heart and the thoughts that entered her mind. As she spoke, she found herself wrestling with rage! By the time she had finished, however, she had come to terms with that human tendency to retaliate, and she spoke to the guard of forgiveness and of the Lord Jesus Christ.

Joseph is another who modeled the right spirit when it came to retaliation. His brothers hated him and sold him into slavery. They made life miserable for him. They didn't care if he died, and fully expected him to do so. Instead, he wound up prime minister of the land that had food when famine struck every other place. When his brothers arrived seeking aid and good, they did not recognize the prime minister as their brother. And when they did learn his identity, they fully expected death. But Joseph said, "You meant evil against me, but God meant it for good" (Gen. 50:20). He not only provided them with food, he invited his father, his brothers, and their families to come and live in the land of Egypt. He, in fact, gave them the choice land of Goshen, which they occupied for over 400 years. No retaliation here, only disciplined self-control.

THE JEWS WHO WERE FREED IN PERSIA

I've taken a little longer setting the stage for the next scene in Esther's story. But hers is a natural when it comes to the subject of getting even.

The Jews in Persia, had been living under the sword of Damocles for months. Death drew closer with every sunset. As the weeks and months rolled along, no doubt they began to see the sneers and hear the sarcastic remarks and experience the growing anti-Semitic mistreatment that had begun with Haman. Those Gentiles licked their chops, looking forward to wiping out the Jews. It was an extermination plot of the worst kind, written into the unchangeable law of the Medes and the Persians. Day after day they lived with this threat, the thought of this horror! Did families talk about it? About how they would face it? Of possible ways to escape it? To save their children? You know they did—wouldn't you? Surely they called upon God to save them. The most devout asked Him to go with them as they faced such a dreadful fate. It was at this juncture, you'll recall, that Esther stepped in, stood tall, and interceded for her people.

Suddenly, one day, the tables turned. The power shifted. Haman, the anti-Semitic official, was impaled on his own gallows, and Mordecai the Jew was given the place of prime minister. A special edict was then written for them, which we looked at in the last chapter:

> . . . the king granted the Jews who were in each and every city the right to assemble and to defend their lives, to destroy, to kill, and to annihilate the entire army of any people or province which might attack them, including children and women, and to plunder their spoil.
>
> Esther 8:11

That's like giving concentration camp prisoners long-overdue rights. It's cutting the barbed wires. It's feeding *them* rather than the guards. It's an unlimited, no-holds-barred edict.

The entire land was turned against them until this edict. And now they're free to retaliate, "to annihilate the entire army of any people or province, including children and women, and to plunder their spoil." What an opportunity for retaliation! Annihilate them! Leave them devastated!

> A copy of the edict to be issued as law in each and every province, was published to all the peoples, so that the Jews should be ready for this day to avenge themselves on their enemies.
>
> Esther 8:13

Don't miss the flashing green light—they were to "be ready to *avenge* themselves!"

Understand, we were allowed to see inside the king's quarters, where Esther and her husband, the king, and Haman had met. But the general public saw none of the above. All they knew was that the heart of the king had changed. They also became aware that the power in the palace had shifted. They had watched the personnel change. And in the midst of all this, the new edict was declared. This was their moment! Someone has said the most dangerous human being on earth is a prisoner who gets hold of a weapon. "This is my chance!" And we have seen and read of accounts where that kind of retaliation happens, and the gross brutality that bursts from the human heart when revenge takes charge.

The English words "avenge" and "vengeance" come to us through the French, and both languages got it from the Latin *vendicare*, which has the same root as "vindicate." Isn't that curious? "Vengeance," which is passion out of control based on hatred, and "vindicate," which is what God claims to do when defending His people, are from the same root—*vendicare*. They carry contrary messages. In order for there to be the restraint of vengeance, self-control must be applied.

I believe that is exactly what we read in the ninth chapter of Esther. I have frequently read or heard the term "bloodbath" applied to the last part of her story. It sounds like human depravity out of control, the rage of revenge gone wild. Thousands of people killed. It is almost as if the Jews picked them off from their windows with delight!

Joyce Baldwin offers helpful insight here:

Though in the Book of Esther the tables had been turned on those who would have killed the Jews, the Jews had behind them all the theological conditioning provided by their scriptures, and their understanding of permission to avenge themselves would have been adjusted accordingly. Instead of having to endure slaughter without any means of self-defence, the new legislation permitted them to fight for one day against those who attacked them and to kill them. The fact that this surprising change in the circumstances had taken place was awe-inspiring. It pointed to a providential ordering of their affairs, not to be taken lightly. To be sure it was wonderful, and a cause of rejoicing, but arrogance and presumption were ruled out, together with all bullying, self-assertive superiority, which in turn would call for God's condemnation and punishment.[55]

In other words, the Jews were allowed to administer self-defense, restraining evil . . . but in doing so, they were to apply great self-control.

Built into the heart of those ancient Jews was a long-term restraint derived from the teachings of the Torah, the holy Scriptures, that held them in check. Let me show you.

Now in the twelfth month (that is, the month Adar), on the thirteenth day when the king's command and edict were about to be executed, on the day when the enemies of the Jews hoped to gain the mastery over them, it was turned to the contrary so that the Jews themselves gained the mastery over those who hated them.

Esther 9:1

The writer refers twice to gaining "the mastery" over one another, emphasizing a switch in who held the upper hand. To begin with, after the passing of Haman's edict, the Gentiles had "gained mastery" over the Jews and waited for the day they could attack! Then the tables turned, and with the passing of Mordecai's edict, the Jews have "gained mastery" over those who would have destroyed them. Certainly, there was the temptation to express their "mastery" without limits, "Take advantage of this opportunity. Let's get even. Get back."

Did they? Well, they certainly defended themselves. In doing so, they inflicted just punishment. But we can't say they were out of control. I'll show you why.

> The Jews assembled in their cities throughout all the provinces of King Ahasuerus to lay hands on those who sought their harm; and no one could stand before them, for the dread of them had fallen on all the peoples.
>
> Esther 9:2

Remember World War II and the death camps? Don't think for a moment that when the barbed wire was cut as the Allied troops swarmed in and the prisoners in the death camps were freed that dread didn't fall on the guards—and for just reason. That's like the scene we find here.

> Even all the princes of the provinces, the satraps, the governors, and those who were doing the king's business assisted the Jews, because the dread of Mordecai had fallen on them. Indeed, Mordecai was great in the king's house, and his fame spread throughout all the provinces; for the man Mordecai became greater and greater.
>
> Thus the Jews struck all their enemies with the sword, killing and destroying; and they did what they pleased to those who hated them. And in Susa the capital the Jews killed and destroyed five hundred men . . .

And then it names several of those who were killed, citing them specifically because they were

> the ten sons of Haman the son of Hammedatha, the Jews' enemy; but they did not lay their hands on the plunder.
>
> Esther 9:3–10

Pay close attention to that last phrase: "*but they did not lay their hands on the plunder.*" They *had* the freedom to take the spoils from those they annihilated—from those who would have annihilated them. But they did not. They defended themselves, but went no further. More importantly, the edict had given them the freedom to kill women and children, but they didn't carry it to that extreme. At least there is nothing recorded in the account to indicate that they did.

> On that day the number of those who were killed in Susa the capital was reported to the king. And the king said to Queen Esther, "The Jews have killed and destroyed five hundred men and the ten sons of Haman in Susa the capital. What then have they done in the rest of the king's provinces! Now what is your petition? It shall even be granted you. And what is your further request? It shall also be done."
>
> Esther 9:11–12

The king seems astonished that the Jews have killed five hundred men in Susa alone. If that is the case, he reflects, how many will they have killed throughout the rest of the provinces? At that point, you might expect the king to say, "That's enough! Touch no one else!" But he trusts Esther.

I think it is noteworthy how significantly this man relies on and respects the counsel of his wife, Esther. He's still the king. But it is obvious that her opinion matters a great deal to him. Her inner strength had been wonderfully displayed in previous hours—the way she handled her concern regarding Haman's wicked plan, the manner in which she expressed compassion for her people, the wisdom shown in her timing of silence as well as speech. Ahasuerus knew she was a woman of enormous character. When that is true, "the heart of her husband trusts in her" (Prov. 31:11). And so he asks if there is anything else he can do for her. What a question! But, again, Esther reveals strength in her response. But don't think for a moment she was soft. This lady has guts!

> Then said Esther, "If it pleases the king, let tomorrow also be granted to the Jews who are in Susa to do according to the edict of today; and let Haman's ten sons be hanged on the gallows."

> So the king commanded that it should be done so; and an edict
> was issued in Susa, Haman's ten sons were hanged.
>
> Esther 9:13–14

The queen asked for one more day in which the Jews could defend themselves. She also asked that Haman's ten sons, who had already been killed, be impaled on the gallows their father had built. What was the point of this, since they were already dead? It was a way of saying publicly, "What these men and their father stood for will never be allowed again!" There's a needed message of fear eloquently communicated in capital punishment.

> And the Jews who were in Susa assembled also on the fourteenth day
> of the month Adar and killed three hundred men in Susa, but they
> did not lay their hands on the plunder.
>
> Esther 9:15

Once again, the Jews defended themselves, but they did not do so without self-control. They deliberately restrained from plundering the property belonging to the dead—another confirmation that they did not kill the women and children, but, instead, left the property for them.

> Now the rest of the Jews who were in the king's provinces assembled,
> to defend their lives and rid themselves of their enemies, and kill 75,000
> of those who hated them; but they did not lay their hands on the
> plunder.
>
> Esther 9:16

The Jews were free to strike back without reservation, in retaliation. But it is clear that they applied self-control. The Jews certainly defended themselves against their enemies, against those who attempted to wipe out their race, but the Jews resisted the temptation to go too far. They had been given permission to take material advantage of their enemies' defeat, but they refused to do that. They held back. Think of it this way: Not only did the Jews gain mastery over their enemies, they gained mastery over themselves.

Before going any further, let me explain how the retaliation syndrome works. On a sheet of paper draw two columns. Title the left column "The Offender." Title the right column "The Offended." The left is the initiator of the offense; the right is the recipient. Fill out each column as follows:

THE OFFENDER	THE OFFENDED
Disapproval begins	Awareness of disapproval
Disapproval intensifies and grows into hatred	Inability to change the thinking of the angry person
Hatred begins to be expressed	Beginning of mistreatment
Extreme punishment becomes a way of life	Inability to defend oneself leads to a sense of helplessness, thoughts of retaliation intensify
And then, one day,	
THE TABLES ARE TURNED!	THE TABLES ARE TURNED!
Fear of revenge from the offended	Opportunity provided to get even
Expectation of revenge	Uncontrolled rage surfaces
Full scale acts of hatred or violence experienced	Retaliate with full-scale vengeance

Take time to compare the lists. Notice the erosion on both sides.

First: *the offender*. What begins as mild disapproval turns to hatred, which leads to a way of life that offers extreme punishment to the person who is the object or target of that anger and hatred. This punishment may take the form of nasty words expressed verbally. It may take the form of ugly letters. It may lead to character assassination. It might even become threatening or culminate in physical violence. We certainly see enough evidence of this in our society.

Then, one day, perhaps even for a brief period of time, the tables are turned. The very first thing that occurs when that happens is fear of revenge from the offended. This escalates to an expectation of vengeance. And last, if the retaliation syndrome runs its normal course and nothing stops it, the original offender experiences full-scale acts of hatred or even violence. The person who was hurt gets back his own in full measure. He gets his "revenge," which is another word for "retaliation."

Second: *the offended.* Initially, this person is aware of disapproval. The offended is unable to change the thinking of the angry person, and begins to experience mistreatment. Unable to defend himself, the offended suffers from a sense of helplessness. At this point, the most natural response is for thoughts of retaliation to begin and intensify. Because the offended can't change the situation, because he can't defend himself, he begins to think, *How can I get back at this person?*

Then, one day, the tables are turned. The enormous cat becomes the mouse. The prisoner gets the gun. The victim gains the upper hand. This provides the opportunity to get even. And if there is nothing to stop him, watch out! The offended retaliates against the offender with full-scale vengeance.

This growth of intensity on both sides is exactly what happened between the populace of Persia and the Jews of Persia. One side experienced an escalating hatred, anti-Semitism run rampant. The other side experienced an increased sense of helplessness and defenseless. Then, one day, the tables were turned. Thankfully, restraint was applied before the fires of revenge got out of control. The normal syndrome of retaliation did not occur.

What is it that stops the retaliation syndrome? We're back where we started at the beginning of this chapter. Only one thing: self-control under the Spirit of God. It's the same kind of self-control we need when we battle with lust and anger, addictions and habits, drugs, alcohol, and gluttony. Without self-control, we yield to whatever the temptation and we go too far.

THE CHRISTIAN WHO IS FREE TODAY

What we need to do is look through the lens of Scripture at God's attitude toward retaliation, as seen in Romans 12. In one sense, the Christian can

me to get back or to get even. I'm suggesting you will discover the same is true for you.

> *Dear Father: Your wisdom is rarely heard in our society . . . and even less is it heeded. You speak truth and it cuts to the heart of the matter. Like in these last few paragraphs. You've gotten the attention of this reader and you won't let her ignore what she's read. Help her. Give her whatever it takes to restrain herself from foolish and carnal reactions. Show her how pleased You would be by her doing the hard thing rather than running to the easy thing . . . by forgiving instead of retaliating . . . by growing closer to Christ through obedience rather than distancing herself from Him through some fleshly, out-of-control excursion.*
>
> *Grow her into a modern-day Esther, Lord, so that she might shine like a star in the midst of this dark and angry generation. As You do that, remove those paintings from the gallery of her memory that drain her energy and steal her peace.*
>
> *I ask this in the name of the One who, though He was insulted and mistreated and abused, refused to retaliate, and forgave us all . . . even Jesus Christ our Redeemer. Amen.*

CHAPTER ELEVEN

After the Ache—Celebrate!

We have journeyed through some pretty dark and dismal times with Esther. There were a few moments we found ourselves expecting the worst and wondering if the king's decree to exterminate all the Jews in every province of Persia might actually happen. Dreadful thought! What could possibly stop it?

And then, as Haman had those enormous gallows constructed on which he planned to impale Mordecai publicly, Esther's cousin and adoptive parent, the future seemed completely bleak. All the while we were questioning what, if anything, Esther could do. She may have been the queen, but no queen (in fact, no one!) was free to walk into the king's presence and negotiate any decision he had made. The familiar "law of the Medes and the Persians" was not merely a proverbial phrase in her day, it was an official principle known throughout the land.

Everything seemed lost . . . and nobody felt it more than the Jews of Persia. Since a date was set for this holocaust to begin, each new dawn only deepened the ache of their hearts. Until . . .

Esther was aroused to action by her faithful and godly guardian,

Mordecai. Ignoring long-standing protocol and refusing to be intimidated by the thought of being put to death in doing so, she courageously stepped into the king's private "war room," expressed her concern for her people (and in doing so, revealed to him for the first time that she, too, was Jewish), exposed the deceptive wickedness of Haman's heart, and only hours later, pled that the decree might somehow be altered—or, at least, defended against. All these things occurred in a relatively brief period of time, but they resulted in a remarkable turning point, not only in the colorful story of Esther but in the dramatic history of the Jews.

The results? Everything changed. The king allowed her interruption and listened compassionately to her pleas. Haman was soon hung on the gallows he had built for Mordecai. Mordecai was promoted to the position Haman vacated, prime minister of Persia. And as we saw in the previous chapter, the Jews were liberated from the fear of extermination by another decree that allowed them to defend themselves from and all who would attempt to harm them. The first verse of Esther 9 says it all:

> . . . on the day when the enemies of the Jews hoped to gain the mas-
> tery over them, it was turned to the contrary so that the Jews them-
> selves gained the mastery over those who hated them.

Wonderful news! Good-bye fear and pain, hello relief and pleasure! Operation celebration kicked in.

If I may jump momentarily from then to now, I think it's necessary to mention something I have noticed among God's family. Most Christians seem to handle pain better than pleasure. For some strange reason we seem to do better with hard days than we do with easy days, with tough times rather than fun times. Stress and anxiety we expect. Reward and relief don't seem natural. Many of our critics would tell us that it is because we operate so much of our lives under self-imposed guilt. They may be right! We somehow anticipate being "punished" for something we've done wrong or failed to do. We weep with those who weep much more easily than rejoice with those who rejoice.

When we take a two-week vacation, most folks need the first week just to begin to enjoy it, often because we're so wound up we don't relax. It takes us that long to give ourselves permission to relax and enjoy the reward of a long year of hard work well done. Too bad celebration comes so slowly!

Deep within our minds there seems to lurk a bad news mentality. Ever noticed that about yourself? If someone says to you, "I want to talk to you before long about something that's been on my mind," what is the first thing that springs to your mind? Is it, *Oh, he wants to tell me something good?* Not on your life. We expect the worst. It's much more likely that you'll find yourself saying, "Why don't you just tell me now, so I don't have to worry about it." Or if someone says, "I've written you a letter. You'll get it in a day or two," your immediate response is, "Oh, no." Rather than a letter of affirmation, we expect confrontation and criticism. Why are we like that? It's as if we resist and run from the positive, since we live in such a negative setting. When will we ever learn to operate in the realm of grace? When will we ever allow ourselves sufficient freedom to really celebrate?

My sister, Luci Swindoll, has this take on it:

> The highest and most desirable state of the soul is to praise God in celebration for being alive. Without perks our lives are easily lost in the world of money, machines, anxiety, or inertia. Our poor, splendid souls! How they fight for food! They have forgotten how to celebrate. They have forgotten to request little perks. Our hurried, stressful, busy lives are unquestionably the most dangerous enemy of celebrating life itself. Somehow we must learn how to achieve momentary slowdowns, and request from God a heightened awareness of the conception that life is a happy thing, a festival to be enjoyed rather than a drudgery to be endured. Life is *full* of perks, if we train ourselves to perceive them.[56]

I honestly do not believe God desires us to grind out our existence in a long tunnel of tasks and responsibilities and deadlines. God has given us joy rather than sadness; He has exchanged our tears for smiles. Yet many still find themselves more comfortable mourning and fretting than rejoicing and celebrating.

LOOKING OVER THE PAST WITH A SIGH

Why is that? I think I know one of the reasons. I believe we do this because we are much more riveted to the past than focused on the future. And being negative by nature, being bad-news people by habit, we tend to pick out of the past the things that make us sigh and let them bleed into the present so that they color and stain our emotions, robbing us of a sense of humor, and making us prematurely grim as well as gray!

Several years ago I decided to *do* something about this, so I wrote an entire book on it, calling it *Laugh Again*. What a therapy! And what a wonderful response from those who read it! My files include many delightful letters from folks who thanked me for the reminder that it's still OK to laugh and enjoy life.

And the stories they included—what fun to read them and smile alongside them! I'll never forget one included in a letter by a woman who was standing at a cosmetics counter in a large department store when a hurried, anxious lady rushed up to the salesclerk who was already waiting on two other customers.

"Do you still have Elizabeth Taylor's *Passion?*" she blurted out.

With quick wit, the saleslady looked over her shoulder and answered back, "If I did, you think I'd be working here?"

When we look back into the past, life stops being fun. The things that make us sigh are at least four in number: people, events, circumstances, and decisions. Let me, rather quickly, elaborate on these.

First: *people of the past.* I'm thinking of people we wronged, and people who wronged us. And because of past sadness connected with wrong relationships or unhappy, unfulfilling, unproductive relationships, our present is marred.

Second: *events of the past.* When we look back, we don't remember the times of celebration, the great birthday parties, memorable wedding anniversaries, the joys of an evening around the fireplace, the pleasures of family togetherness. You know what we remember? We remember things like earthquakes or tornadoes or hurricanes or floods. We can even state the dates and often the hour!

"Three years ago today at 5:16 A.M., we had a 5.6 shaker." "Today's the anniversary of Hurricane Andrew." "Remember the great flood of '52?" Granted, these dates have significance for those who lived through the disaster or for those who lost loved ones. But if we constantly measure our lives only by these events, our outlook becomes fearful and our attitude tends to be negative.

Third: *circumstances of the past.* Conversations. Difficult situations. Relational barriers. Divorce conflicts. Racial injustices. Standing toe-to-toe with one of our teenagers. A jobless interlude. These serve as perpetual anchors, holding our joy in check.

Fourth: *decisions of the past.* This may be the worst of the four. There isn't a person reading these lines who hasn't made wrong decisions, hurried and costly decisions, foolish decisions. Who hasn't made weak decisions, who hasn't gone too far . . . or not far enough? So, today we're all hung up because we are *snagged* on some decision of the past—a decision which, in fact, we cannot change!

The enemy of our souls loves to taunt us with these past failures, wrongs, disappointments, disasters, and calamities. And if we let him continue doing this, our life becomes a long and dark tunnel, with very little light at the end.

Fortunately, God has given us a magnificent solution that *can* make a difference. I call these fourteen words the secret of celebrating life.

> . . . forgetting what lies behind and reaching forward to what lies ahead, I press on. . . .
>
> Philippians 3:13–14

Do you have any idea what Paul's philosophy will do to your whole life? It will turn you into a much more lighthearted celebrant. You will discover that you mourn and sigh less, and you begin to laugh at life with God by your side.

ACKNOWLEDGING THE PRESENT WITH A CELEBRATION

Even in Esther's story, the past with all its sadness did not eclipse their joy, once things turned around. By now you know this story well: how the plot thickened, how disaster seemed to be written across every Jewish life, how doom was predicted so clearly, so eloquently . . . and how God changed the events to turn wrong into right.

Let's return to one detail we can't afford to overlook:

> . . . therefore Haman sought to destroy all the Jews, the people of Mordecai, who were throughout the whole kingdom of Ahasuerus.
>
> In the first month, which is the month Nisan, in the twelfth year of King Ahasuerus, Pur, that is the lot, was cast before Haman from day to day, from month to month, until the twelfth month, that is the month Adar.
>
> Esther 3:6–7

When Haman was trying to decide when to carry out his plot to exterminate the Jews, he relied on the ancient custom of casting lots. A lot was called *Pur*. And in the casting of the lots, he came upon a date: the thirteenth of Adar. What interests me is not only the date but the original name of the lot, *Pur*. C. F. Keil states that *Pur* ". . . is an Old-Persian word meaning lot."[57]

In English, we usually form the plural of a word by adding "s" or "es." In Hebrew and its sister language Aramaic, a singular term is turned into plural by adding "im." Thus, the Hebrew plural for cherub is not cherubs but *cherubim*. The plural for seraph, another kind of angel, is not seraphs but *seraphim*. The multiple forms of the god Baal is not Baals but *Baalim*. So if we were to pluralize *Pur*, making the lot represent lots, it would be *Purim*.

So Haman, in casting the Purim, settled upon a certain day that would rid the kingdom of the Jews.

> And letters were sent by couriers to all the king's provinces to destroy, to kill, and to annihilate all the Jews, both young and old, women and children, in one day, the thirteenth day of the twelfth month, which is the month Adar, and to seize their possession as plunder.
>
> Esther 3:13

We know, of course, that the tables were soon turned. Haman's anti-Semitism was uncovered and disclosed to the king, and Esther's heart won the king's mind. And the king made the decision not only to kill Haman, but to wipe the slate clean and neutralize the sentence of death for the Jews by enabling them to defend themselves.

> This was done on the thirteenth day of the month Adar [the very day they were originally to have died] and on the fourteenth day they rested and made it a day of feasting and rejoicing.
>
> Esther 9:17

In honor of this remarkable change of events, the Jews declared a day of celebration, called, appropriately, the Feast of Purim. And it is still celebrated by the Jews to this day. What was going to be their death turned and became their hope for life in the future, their cause for celebration. I find it interesting that in this case, their past caused them to celebrate, not grieve. This is one of the reasons our holidays, based on wonderful memories, are such celebrative times. In those cases, the memory of some past event becomes the ground for celebration.

In his later years, Vance Havner, the evangelist, wrote a little book entitled *It Is Toward Evening*. In it he tells the unforgettable story of a little town in Alabama where the major livelihood was raising cotton. One year, as it appeared that there would be a bumper crop, the boll weevil invaded, devastated the crop, and destroyed the economy of that little town.

Farmers, however, are an ingenious lot, and these particular farmers were determined not to simply sit back and move into the poorhouse. One man got the idea of planting peanuts instead. (Boll weevils don't like peanuts!) Another farmer decided to plant yet another kind of crop, and others followed suit. Before long, bumper crops of peanuts and other produce began to repair the economy of this town. Interestingly, the town later came to be known as Enterprise, Alabama. And do you know what they did? *They erected a monument to the boll weevil!*

As Havner writes insightfully:

> "All things work together for good" to the Christian, even our boll weevil experiences. Sometimes we settle into a humdrum routine as monotonous as growing cotton year after year. Then God sends the

boll weevil; He jolts us out of our groove, and we must find new ways to live. Financial reverses, great bereavement, physical infirmity, loss of position—how many have been driven by trouble to be better husbandmen and to bring forth far finer fruit from their souls! The best thing that ever happened to some of us was the coming of our "boll weevil." Without that we might still have been a "cotton sharecropper."[58]

Talk about how to take the pain out of our past! Each of us has had our own boll weevil experience. It interrupted the pleasures of our life. It stole our joy. It had the audacity to invade without invitation, and it probably came by surprise. Chances are good it *devastated* our faith at the time. We were cut down to size. The lot was cast. But did it end our days? We didn't die! On the contrary, in many cases, it became our turning point toward real living! The problem occurs when we don't build our monument, when we don't establish our own Purim, our plan for celebrating.

Are you still living in the sigh and the pain of all the sadness that comes over you when you remember the brokenness? That's what this is about. This isn't just a story about some ancient feast in Persia. God has given us His Word not simply to teach us dates and learn about Hebrew history. He's given us His Word to reconstruct our lives, to build monuments where we once wept and bled, where our lives were hurt and our hearts ached, when we felt displaced and devastated. But forgetting that which lies behind and moving forward toward that which lies ahead . . . this is the way we press on!

This doesn't mean we just forget the past, proclaiming, "Oh yeah. It was awful." Instead, we *build a monument!* Celebrate the feast! During such celebrations, we pass along the lessons that led to the changes and results in the maturing experiences that were so essential in our lives and so different from when we were just a bunch of cotton sharecroppers.

When I read verses 17, 18, and 19 of chapter 9 in Esther, I smile. Why? Because I'm reading about a people who decided, "Let's name this day a day for a holiday. Let's call it Purim." Which could be translated, "In your face, Haman! . . . Here's to our God!" (another outrageous Swindoll paraphrase).

This was done on the thirteenth day of the month Adar, and on the fourteenth day they rested and made it a day of feasting and rejoicing.

But the Jews who were in Susa assembled on the thirteenth and the fourteenth of the same month, and they rested on the fifteenth day and made it a day of feasting and rejoicing.

Therefore the Jews of the rural areas, who live in the rural towns, make the fourteenth day of the month Adar a holiday for rejoicing and feasting and sending portions of food to one another.

Esther 9:17–19

This reminds me of the spontaneous celebration that became the first Thanksgiving in the New World. After enduring the bitterness of winter, the early colonists decided to hold a feast, celebrating their survival and giving thanks to God for His protection and provisions throughout the past months. It was a spontaneous celebration of praise. It was our forebears' Purim. God had turned their hardship and sorrow and pain into gratitude and health and joy. This early feast officially became Thanksgiving when the governor of Massachusetts declared it so.

In verses 20 through 28 of Esther 9, we find the Feast of Purim becoming official, as recorded by Mordecai who, quite possibly, wrote the book of Esther. Read these words as if you're reading them etched in stone on some memorial site:

Then Mordecai recorded these events, and he sent letters to all the Jews who were in all the provinces of King Ahasuerus, both near and far, obliging them to celebrate the fourteenth day of the month Adar, and the fifteenth day of the same month, annually, because on those days the Jews rid themselves of their enemies, and it was a month which was turned for them from sorrow into gladness and from mourning into a holiday; that they should make them days of feasting and rejoicing and sending portions of food to one another and gifts to the poor.

Thus the Jews undertook what they had started to do, and what Mordecai had written to them. For Haman the son of Hammedatha, the Agagite, the adversary of all the Jews, had schemed against the

Jews to destroy them, and had cast Pur, that is the lot, to disturb them and destroy them.

But when it came to the king's attention, he commanded by letter that his wicked scheme which he had devised against the Jews, should return on his own head, and that he and his sons should be hanged on the gallows. Therefore they called these days Purim after the name Pur. And because of the instructions in this letter, both what they had seen in this regard and what had happened to them, the Jews established and made a custom for themselves, and for their descendants, and for all those who allied themselves with them, so that they should not fail to celebrate these two days according to their regulation, and according to their appointed time annually.

Esther 9:20–27

So it was to be an annual holiday. Two holidays really, the fourteenth and the fifteenth. And notice the reason for the holiday: "because on those days the Jews rid themselves of their enemies, and it was a month which was turned for them from sorrow into gladness and from mourning into a holiday. . . ."(Esther 9:22).

You see, they knew they were going to die. They knew it was coming . . . *until Almighty God sovereignly intervened.* And now they chose the very days when they would have been annihilated and exterminated, and they turned those days from sadness and mourning to rejoicing and celebration to acknowledge the change of events.

Ask many people what the Book of Esther represents, and they will tell you it's a book of tragedy. They will tell you it's the early holocaust. But you and I know better. In fact, there's no holocaust in Esther. There's a threat of holocaust, but it never happens.

Do you know this is the only book the Jews can turn to to find roots for their holidays of Purim? Do you know that, to this day, when they read from the scrolls of Esther, that little children come dressed in costumes and adults dress up as well. The atmosphere is like an old-time melodrama. Everyone cheers the hero and heroine (Mordecai and Esther) and they boo and hiss and stomp their feet when the name of Haman is mentioned. It's not a reenactment of a tragedy; it's a celebration of triumph. And that's exactly as God planned it.

> So these days were to be remembered and celebrated throughout every generation, every family, every province, and every city; and these days of Purim were not to fail from among the Jews, or their memory fade from their descendants.
>
> Esther 9:28

If this official celebration of Purim had not been established, what happened during Esther's lifetime would have been forgotten within two or three generations. If you doubt this, think of what it is like talking to today's generation about World War I or World War II or the Korean War. I've done it, I know. They have this blank stare. They have absolutely no memory of these years in our history and so they listen with casual interest, but most of them lack any sense of its significance. That's why it is important to "celebrate" events like Memorial Day, Independence Day, Armistice Day, and Thanksgiving Day. Our children and grandchildren have no memory of them . . . but it's important that they *remember* them, nevertheless.

We who have visited Holocaust memorials know how moving such sites can be. Those trees planted alongside the building in Jerusalem housing the horrible memories, each tree representing courageous men and woman, who aided the Jews—what tearful but gallant reminders. Yet, how essential we remember, lest we forget, and, perish the thought, live to see such horrors repeated. Visiting sites like Gettysburg and Pearl Harbor and Dachau is invaluable to all of us.

Within another generation, Vietnam will just be another place on the map in Southeast Asia. There will be no memory in the minds of the young. There will be no sense of anguish, no understanding of what it did to our nation, no sadness over the men and women who sacrificially fought and many who died there. But we can keep remembrance alive by "celebrating" with quiet honor the events of that time.

This is one of the reasons Cynthia and I appreciate returning at least annually to our capital, Washington, D.C. Our nation's life is measured out and relived there in memorials and monuments, celebrating the great moments and events of our history—tragic and triumphant. The Washington Monument. The Lincoln Memorial. The Jefferson Memorial. The Vietnam Memorial. The Iwo Jima Monument in honor of World War II. Those white crosses standing like silent sentries in Arlington Cemetery. The Tomb of the Unknown Solider. The list goes on and on.

Memorials are places provided for us to stand and be quiet, to read and especially to reflect, and to pass on to the next generation the roots of a nation's heritage. They give the present significance because they give the past perspective.

One of my main fears for our present rapid-paced life and lifestyle is that we have so few memorials, so few monuments, even mental monuments. Life is lived in the fast lane. Superficial decisions. Hurry-up childhoods. Quick money. Overnight successes. Fast action. Strong competition. So little time spent stopping and recording segments of our lives in a journal. So little emphasis on listening and learning and honoring.

A divorce breaks and wounds a family deeply . . . and life rushes on. A young woman gets an abortion . . . and life speeds on. A business fails . . . and life goes on. There's a political scandal . . . and life speeds on. A death or a heartache comes, and before long it's swept up in the whirlwind of activity . . . and life goes right on as a nation shrugs rather than grieves. A death or a heartache comes, and before long it's swept up in the whirlwind of activity . . . and grass grows over a grave as life goes on. And we're left with the anguish of a blurred memory, but no lasting perspective, no enduring wisdom.

In order to have perspective, we must have monuments and memorials, places to return to and learn from and talk about and pass on. If we don't, we are destined to live rootless, fast-lane lives without much significance and all-too-seldom celebrations.

Worst of all, our children learn little, often nothing, from our failures, our brokenness, and our sorrows. If anything, they learn only to hate like we hated or to get revenge like we sought to do or simply to drink themselves to sleep like so many choose to do.

Esther determined it wouldn't be like that in her day.

And the command of Esther established these customs for Purim, and it was written in the book.

Esther 9:32

I shout a loud "Thank you!" to our heroine, Esther, at this juncture. She didn't call attention to herself when she "established these customs," she gave her people a lasting reminder that God is faithful as He keeps His promises and preserves His people. Hat's off to you, Queen Esther. May your noble tribe increase!

FACING THE FUTURE WITH A REMINDER

All of us, when looking back, see sadness and remorse and nothing else, unless perspective is provided. Unless we gain some kind of perspective, we will do nothing but sigh and grieve over our past. We'll weep through the night, but there will be no song in the morning.

In light of that, I close this chapter with a suggestion and a warning. My suggestion is that *each one of us raise up our own memorials*—mental monuments that turn tragedies into triumphs.

Webster says a *monument* is "a lasting evidence of something or some-one notable." He also defines a *memorial* as something that "serves to pre-serve remembrance, a commemoration."

Think back for a moment to Havner's story of the coming of the boll weevil. Personalize that event by returning to your own crop failure or disaster. Have you built a monument to it? It may be too close and too raw for you to do it today, but don't spend the rest of your life licking your wounds over yesteryear or you will experience a grim future. Instead, ask yourself, "What did I learn from it?"

You can't change it, it's over. Maybe you should have known better or you ought to have done something differently. But forget about the *shoulds*, *woulds*, and *oughts*. What did you learn from it? Get specific. Write it down. Pass on the wisdom gleaned from your own disaster.

Now, here's the warning: *Don't turn the memorial into a shrine.*

We don't need human-failure shrines any more than we need literal pieces of the cross. We need God-honoring memorials. God has given us just such a memorial in the Communion—the bread and the cup. Now, that's the memorial of the cross worth celebrating! He left it as a legacy for people of faith. But it isn't the symbols we worship. We don't bow before the table where they're served. That's why we say that we "celebrate" Communion. We celebrate the memory and the significance, really the triumph of the cross.

What we need today is an answer to the ache of life, an answer to the Hamans whose shadows have crossed our lives and could have finished us off, and to the would-have-been holocausts that might well have devastated our existence. So take that past person, event, circumstance, or decision and creatively construct your own private memorial. Think through, then record the lessons you learned from it, and pass them on and on and on. The Feast of Purim lives on because the queen determined its lessons would never be forgotten among the Jews.

Esther is a story of triumph that grew out of tragedy, ecstasy out of agony, celebration out of devastation.

Yours can be the same.

CHAPTER TWELVE

In the End, God Wins

This has been a book about Esther, one of the great women in the illustrious history of her people, the Jews. Clearly, she was raised up to fill a role as the queen of Persia that proved crucial at a time when the lives of many hung in the balance. Indeed, as her mentor and faithful guardian reminded her, she "attained royalty for such a time as this" (Esther 4:14). What a prominent figure she was!

We have found it interesting, however, that while she is highly significant in the turning points of history recorded on the sacred page of the Scriptures, she does not dominate every scene of the story. On the contrary, she is often eclipsed by other people and events that are interwoven through these chapters.

For example, it isn't until we are well into the second chapter of the book that bears her name that we read of her for the first time. And as the story unfolds, she reappears from time to time for important reasons, only to be hidden from view again as she steps back into the shadows of the palace. Following the same pattern, she reenters the story toward the end as she makes her requests to her husband the king (9:12–13) then later as she establishes the Purim memorial (9:29-32), only to depart for the last time and not return through the remainder of the book. Not even her name appears in the closing chapter of Esther. Mordecai is prominent, her husband, the king, as well, but not Esther. Her influence, of course, continues to be felt, but that's it. She has exited before the final scene and will not be back, even for a closing curtain call.

Without wanting to make more of this than is warranted, I do think it's appropriate to mention that "the power of a woman" (which I emphasized in my introduction) does not always require her constant physical presence. Esther quietly comes onto the scene, somewhat reluctantly allows herself to be escorted to the palace, but never really dominates any situation even after becoming queen. She does step up, when urged by Mordecai, and plays an essential role in changing the king's thinking, no question. And when invited to give her opinion or speak her mind, Esther did so, occasionally with enormous passion. But none of this ever seemed overly aggressive or inappropriately brash.

It's this elegant touch of restraint I admire as much as anything in Esther, which prompted me to borrow from Proverbs 31:25 in choosing the title for my book, *Esther: A Woman of Strength and Dignity*. Her strength is revealed as much in her restraints as in her responses, and her dignity as much in her humility as in her integrity. Her quiet confidence in God, her teachable trust in Mordecai, her gracious respect for Ahasuerus, her husband, are qualities that impact the story of her life, even though she, herself, is not filling every scene with her presence and instructions and leadership.

We can only imagine her gratitude at the end of the day, after encountering her husband and later confronting Haman. We can feel the heat of her patriotism as she established Purim as a Jewish celebration. And now, as we witness the climax of her story, where Mordecai is acknowledged as a man of greatness (10:2), we can imagine her smiling with true satisfaction. Why? Because God has had His way! Good has triumphed over evil. Hope has dispelled fear. What joy it must have brought this fine woman to realize, deep within her soul, that the Lord used her to accomplish His grand and glorious plan!

This is as good a time as any to state that one of the great themes of

Christianity is triumphant hope. Not just hope as in a distant, vague dream, but *triumphant* hope, the kind of hope where all things end right. In the midst of the struggles and the storms and the sufferings of life, we can advance our thoughts beyond today and see relief . . . triumph . . . victory. Because, in the end, God does indeed win.

Think that through. All earthly woes, all financial pressures, all emotional trauma, all physical disabilities and handicaps, all domestic conflicts, all international wars and frightening rumors of wars, all demonic oppressions and satanic attacks, All that ends. And we will be with Him who wins! And that means nothing but harmony and unity and victory and joy and praise and delight.

We'll be changed down inside. We'll have new natures. We'll have new minds. We'll have new bodies. We'll have the joy of living forever and ever in praise and adoration of our God.

In the end, God comes out on top. His plan prevails. That's why I love the story of Esther. Not only does it have a great plot that keeps you on the edge of your seat, but when it comes to the final scene, things turn out right. Things end well. God wins!

Doesn't it drive you nuts to go to a movie that just stops? You walk out thinking, *Well, I guess this is the intermission.* But, you know it's the end! Or the end of a book that just leaves you empty, wondering. You keep turning, thinking maybe after a few blank pages there'll be a better ending. But it's not there. If you're like me, you like things that wrap up neatly, that have a triumphant, God-honoring ending. And if you're like me, you love it when truth wins out, when right wins over wrong, when good reigns supreme. Again, that's what I like so much about Esther.

A FINAL GLIMPSE AT THE STORY AFTER THE FACT

Now King Ahasuerus laid a tribute on the land and on the coastlands of the sea. And all the accomplishments of his authority and strength, and the full account of the greatness of Mordecai, to which the king advanced him, are they not written in the Book of the Chronicles of the Kings of Media and Persia? For Mordecai the Jew was second only to King Ahasuerus and great among the Jews, and in favor with the multitude of his kinsmen, one who sought the good of his people and one who spoke for the welfare of his whole nation.

Esther 10:1–3

End of the book. And it ends like it ought to end.

What do we have here? Well, to begin with, we have the same king that we started with, King Ahasuerus. We have the same kingdom, where he reigns from India to Ethiopia, over 127 provinces. That hasn't changed. We have the same country, Persia, and the same capital city, Susa.

But some things have changed. Vashti is no longer queen; Esther is queen. And she is a queen who has won her husband's overwhelming respect and loyalty. Haman was once second in command, but he is gone forever. Mordecai is alive and well. Wicked plans have been thwarted. Corruption has been rooted out. Evil has been fully dealt with.

To make matters even better, Mordecai has been promoted by the king, and he is now second in command, "second only to King Ahasuerus." Verse 3 yields some helpful information that explains why Mordecai is described as a man of "greatness" in verse 2.

We're told four things about him. First, he "was great among the Jews." Second, he was "in favor with the multitude of his kinsmen." Third, he "sought the good of his people." And fourth, he "spoke for the welfare of his whole nation." Not too shabby an epitaph.

If all's well that ends well, we'd have to agree, this is "well." You have to remember, this was a Gentile country where Gentiles ruled. The Jews who lived here were only a remnant, and they were here only by the permission of the government. They could have been killed when their homeland was conquered, but they were allowed to live—and permitted to live on in this land of Persia. Now, to our amazement, and certainly to the amazement of many of the people of Persia—both Jew and Gentile—a Jew is second in command to King Ahasuerus.

The one who is exalted to the place of authority in Persia is a surprising choice. Who would have ever guessed that a Jew would become the prime minister in a Gentile land? It would have made the headlines of the *Susa*

Daily Sun: "GENTILE KING CHOOSES NEW PRIME MINISTER—A JEW!" That's the surprising part.

It doesn't say, "King Ahasuerus, a Gentile, promoted Mordecai, the Jew." verse 3. Of course not. Because being a Gentile didn't make news. Being a Jew did. That's surprising. But, you see, God is the One in charge, not the king!

All this brings me to three overall observations which yield three principles for our own lives from this ancient book.

The first principle: *When God wins, the people He uses are often unexpected.*

This reminds me of one of my all-time favorite psalms, Psalm 78, which concludes with this comment about David.

> He [God] also chose David His servant,
> And took him from the sheepfolds;
> From the care of the ewes with suckling lambs He brought him,
> To shepherd Jacob His people,
> And Israel His inheritance.
> So he shepherded them according to the integrity of his heart,
> And guided them with his skillful hands.
>
> Psalm 78:70-72

What a surprise! For almost forty years the Israelites had experienced the reign of a king who was tall, dark, and probably handsome, King Saul, who, though he failed in character, at least looked regal. The people had selected Saul, partly because of his appearance. They became accustomed to such a stature. Until God slipped His hand into the ranks of the Jews and picked an unknown young shepherd. Surprising choice.

Or, consider another unexpected choice. If you wanted to lead an exodus of two million people out of Egypt, who would you choose to confront Pharaoh—a Jew or a fellow Egyptian? Be honest, now. And if you chose a Jew, would you choose a man with murder on his record? And would he be eighty years old? And would you select a leather-skinned shepherd who hadn't been in a big city for forty years? See, the further you look, the more surprising it gets. Moses' resumé was pretty unimpressive: "Worked for father-in-law as shepherd for past 40 years." He was an over-the-hill Bedouin.

Would you have chosen a harlot to hide the spies? Would you have chosen a defecting, rebellious prophet to lead the Greater Nineveh Evangelistic Crusade? Would you have chosen a former Christian-hating Pharisee to model grace and to write most of the New Testament? Would you have chosen a man who denied Jesus (three times!) as the major spokesman for the early church?

But, you see, God does surprising things. That's why He lifts a no-name from the gate of the king and makes him a prime minister. God delights in lifting up nobodies and using them as somebodies. As Paul writes to the Corinthians, "not many mighty, not many noble," in other words, not many blue bloods are chosen. He has chosen the despised and many of the losers of the world to follow the One who died on a cross.

This opens the door to the second principle: *When God wins, the qualities He upholds are usually unpretentious.* Mordecai doesn't seem to have a "kingly look" about him. He doesn't fit well on a throne. There is nothing said here or elsewhere that Mordecai looked good in royal robes. But that's the point: God uses humble people. Esther herself was from humble means. We never read of her being highly educated or eloquent of speech or greatly gifted.

Listen to what is said of our Lord Jesus when He came from heaven to earth as a little baby in a manger.

> Have this attitude in yourselves which was also in Christ Jesus, who, although He existed in the form of God, did not regard equality with God a thing to be grasped, but *[But* when God said to His Son, "It's time to go,"] [He] emptied Himself, taking the form of a bond-servant, and being made in the likeness of men. [That's the incarnation. That's when God became man.] And being found in appearance as a man, He humbled Himself by becoming obedient to the point of death, even death on a cross.
>
> Philippians 2:5–8

That was the worst kind of death. That was capital punishment for common criminals. It does say, in the next verse, that God also has "highly exalted Him," and that, ultimately, "at the name of Jesus every knee should bow" (Phil. 2:9-10). But in order to get to that triumphant point, He remained humble and became obedient.

Remember, when God wins, the qualities that He upholds are unassuming and unpretentious.

And by the way, remember, humility is not how you dress, it is not the money you make, it is not where you live, it's not what you drive, it is not even how you look. We're never once commanded by God to "look" humble. Humility is an attitude. It is an attitude of the heart. An attitude of the mind. It is knowing your proper place. Never talking down or looking down because someone may be of a financial level less than yours. It is knowing your role and fulfilling it for God's glory and praise. I repeat, it is an attitude. "Have this *attitude* in yourselves which was also in Christ Jesus" (Phil 2:5, emphasis mine).

If you want to know how that works itself out in your life, go back two verses earlier in Philippians 2:

> Do nothing from selfishness or empty conceit, but with humility of mind let each of you regard one another as more important than himself; do not merely look out for your own personal interests, but also for the interests of others.
>
> Philippians 2:3–4

Have the attitude Christ had, who emptied Himself of the voluntary and independent use of His divine attributes. There is no quality more godlike than humility. (I have the feeling Esther learned humility from Mordecai, who modeled it consistently as she was growing up.)

Remember that when the next promotion comes. Remember that when God selects you as one of His unique spokespersons and places you in a position where the public looks up to you and listens to you. Remember the importance of humility of heart and mind. Nothing is more admirable, more godlike than being willing to live out true humility . . . without calling attention to it.

These thoughts on true humility remind me of an apocryphal story I read recently, about a young man named Walter . . .

who went to work for the largest corporation in the world. The personnel director told Walter he must start at the bottom and work his way up, so he began work in the mailroom. Walter liked his job, but often daydreamed about what it would be like to be an executive, the president, maybe even chairman of the board!

One day as Walter was dividing the mail, he saw a cockroach in the corner of the room. He walked over to step on it. Walter heard a tiny voice crying out, "Don't kill me! I'm Milton the cockroach, and if you spare me I'll grant you all your wishes." Walter agreed that was a good arrangement, and he spared Milton's life.

Walter's first wish was to leave the mailroom and become a vice president, so Milton granted him the wish. In fact, Milton granted wish after wish until finally Walter was the chairman of the board of the largest corporation in the whole world, with an office on the top floor of the tallest building in the whole world. Everyone looked up to Walter and he was very happy. Walter often said to himself, "I'm Walter, and I'm at the top. No one is bigger or more important than me."

Then one day Walter heard footsteps on the roof, and went out to find a small boy on his knees, praying. "Are you praying to Walter?" he asked—after all, he was the chairman of the board of the largest corporation in the world. The boy replied, "Oh, no. No, I'm praying to God."

Walter was quite disturbed by this turn of events, so he returned to his office and sent for Milton the cockroach. "I have another wish," he told Milton. "I want to be like God." And so Milton granted Walter's wish. The next day Walter was back in the mailroom.[59]

The way up is down. The place of highest exaltation, as we see in the Lord Jesus Christ, is a place of self-emptying humility. It's not a phony-baloney style of fake piety. It's true humility of mind. It's putting the other person first. It's sharing and sharing alike. It is giving up as well as building up. It is enjoying the pleasures of another's promotion. It is applauding God's hand in other lives. It is quickly forgetting one's own clippings. It is being like Mordecai, who lived "in favor with the multitude his kinsmen, one who sought the good of his people." Best of all, it is being like Christ.

The one who is highly esteemed by others represents vast vision. Don't miss something important stated here about Mordecai. He was "one who spoke for the welfare of his whole nation." Literally, the sentence reads, "He spoke *shalom*. . . ." That's the ancient word for "peace." Mordecai "spoke peace."

This brings us to our third principle: *When God wins, the message He honors is a universal message.* Mordecai's world was vast; it was not limited to his own immediate family, or even to his own familiar neighborhood. Nor was it limited to Susa where he lived, where the king's throne room was located. It wasn't limited to 15 or 20 provinces he preferred. It spread over all 127. And he spoke "*shalom*" to the entire country.

Shalom is an ancient word for health and security and material plenty. It is a word of greatest delight among the Jews. He spread a wholesome message of hope and security to all the people, which certainly pleased the Lord. Why? Because God has the whole world on His heart, every tongue and tribe and nation. Remember His Son's closing commission? "Go therefore and make disciples of all the nations. . . . (Matt. 28:19).

Unfortunately, the world we live in does not operate on any of these three principles. For example, when the world selects its major players, the criteria are much different. We look for the sharp, the capable, the competent, the strong. We look for those who sound good and look good and have an excellent, broad education and fit the mold of an impressive leader. We do not look for the unexpected; we're not that open to the surprising.

When the world looks for qualities that will get the job done, the externals get the nod. We like people with charisma, people who have pizzazz, who can put up a good front. I've noticed in the past twenty-plus years, we are looking less and less for integrity and honor and true character in a president. We look for people who look good on television, people who can debate an opponent with great ease and little facial sweat, who can compromise enough to please just about everyone. We prefer the externals. Character we'll do without if we have to, but not those externals. But God passes up the externals and looks for the humble of heart!

We live in a world where we take care of our own. We look out for number one. But God's plan encompasses everyone. Every nation. Every race. All cultures. Huge, highly developed countries, but not excluding the small, struggling ones. His message of *shalom* through faith in Christ is universal. Unlimited. Without prejudice. Vast!

A GLORIOUS HOPE FOR THE CHRISTIAN
AT ALL TIMES

Our God continues to be a God of surprises. Nowhere is that more evident than in the story of Esther. He elevated an unknown young woman, an orphan, a Jew, to the Persian throne. He moved in the heart of a powerful, moody, stubborn, unbelieving Gentile king. He turned the evil plan of an anti-Semitic official on its head and worked it to His own ends. He used a humble Jew in exile to change the entire history of a kingdom and a people.

But don't think for a moment that God is finished with surprises! He continues to get our attention by using the "surprise method." Just look back a few years. Anything surprising happen? What hope this gives us!

God not only does the unexpected, He upholds the unpretentious. Do you know what that allows us to do? It allows us to take a universal message wherever we go . . . and it fits. You can step into the streets in an urban ghetto or you can walk into the palace of kings, and it fits. You can take a message to English-speaking people or go halfway around the globe to a culture and language altogether different, and it fits. His message is a universal message. And so the hope we have is a hope of *shalom* for the whole world!

And in the end never forget, He wins. Whether you believe it or not, God wins. Whether you accept it or not, God wins. Whether you even return to Him in repentance, God wins. Whether you bow before Him as Savior and Lord, *God still wins.*

Esther and Mordecai could have proclaimed with the apostle Paul,

> I have fought the good fight, I have finished the course, I have kept
> the faith; in the future there is laid up for me the crown of righteous-
> ness, which the Lord, the righteous Judge, will award to me on that
> day; and not only to me, but also to all who have loved His appearing.
>
> 2 Timothy 4:7–8

Right at the end of his life, the great apostle said, in effect, "And the best is yet to come. Of all things, He not only blessed me with His glorious gospel in my life, He waits to crown faithful service after my death. What a glorious hope is mine!"

In the end, He wins—as do all who serve Him. Not "pie in the sky by and by"; but a permanent home in heaven, where we will know and experience an eternal existence of *shalom!*

One man has written,

> It is strange how when we imagine heaven, we think of it as somehow
> shadowy. We color it with the tints of moonlight, sleep, and the faces
> of the dead. But there are no shades there; there is the substance of
> joy, and the vitality of action. [60]

"The substance of joy and the vitality of action." Now, that's what I call a hope worth claiming! That's our future home, that is, those of us who know Christ. That's where all arguments, suffering, disabilities, handicaps, brokenness, losses, tears, and tragedies will cease. That's where God will reign triumphant, in glory and majesty. That's where Christ will be the light and where we shall see Him as He is. No longer by faith—but by sight. No longer in hope but in absolute reality.

> *Lord, bring us back to the ancient message Esther portrays for us in her*
> *book. It's the same one that Jesus Christ not only declared but modeled.*
> *Bring us back to the One who is indeed our victor. Show us the impor-*
> *tance of a humble spirit and true character. Give us a sense of satisfaction*

in being in Your plan, regardless of what that may mean for us on this earth. Give us the faith to trust You, even when You seem removed and distant. Fill us with hope as we anticipate the end that is sure to come. In the meantime, dear Father, make us responsible people who, like Esther, have been placed in our particular circumstances "for such a time as this," that we might carry Your message to a whole world. Give us her kind of courage and strength and dignity. And in that process, Lord, keep us from relying on our own ingenuity and determination. Remind us again and again that in the end, You win! May our hope rest firmly in Your Son Jesus Christ, in whose strong name I pray. Amen.

CONCLUSION

Esther: A Woman of Strength & Dignity

Esther. What a great lady! And what a remarkable story is contained in the biblical book that bears her name. What enduring principles she leaves in her legacy!

As we have seen in these twelve chapters, her story has all the ingredients of the traditional short story: a dramatic beginning, a suspenseful plot, a villain, a hero, a damsel in distress, and a surprising twist of events that leads to a climax where right triumphs over wrong, and everybody "lives happily ever after." Well, at least it seemed that way as the closing lines show Mordecai appropriately rewarded for his righteous deeds and the people applauding his promotion as he spoke for the welfare of all the Jews (10:3). In Esther's day, everybody around her had smiles on their faces.

Being an optimist, I enjoy stories that end like hers. I love it when truth wins out, when wicked schemes are exposed, and someone in authority uses that authority to stamp out the evil and reward the good.

But about the time I start drifting off into that dreamlike mentality, I'm jolted back to my senses with a sudden blast of reality. Sin reemerges. As a Haman is impaled on the gallows and we're cheering the arrival of long-awaited justice, another deceiver is sure to come on the scene with wicked intentions . . . and we're back into it all over again.

One cruel dictator is exposed, caught, and removed . . . yet another is always waiting in the wings. One war is ended as bruised and broken people rejoice in their relief . . . but it isn't long before another breaks out on another part of the globe as selfishness, pride, and stubbornness join forces against those who cannot defend themselves. As long as depravity is present, we can expect this replay of heartbreaking misery.

But there's good news in the midst of all this, and we have Esther to thank for the reminder. God may seem distant and uninvolved, but He is neither. He's very much at work—raising up a man of character like Mordecai who faithfully invests himself in others, believing that God may someday choose to use the one being trained in righteousness. And while we're looking at the bright side, God is also preparing another woman of courage, as He did Esther, to play a role of immense importance, which no other person but she can accomplish.

As we learned in our study of Esther's story, His hand moves invisibly, yet with invincibility, bringing His sovereign plan to completion. It includes haunting delays that seem unfair, human decisions that lack compassion, harmful deeds that bring other anguish, and hurtful disappointments that make us question God's goodness. Nevertheless, He pursues with persistence and He refuses to be distracted. In the end, I repeat, God wins. What great comfort that brings!

ENDNOTES

INTRODUCTION

1. Ray Stedman, *The Queen and I, Studies in Esther* (Waco, Tex.: Word Books, 1977), 7.

CHAPTER I

2. Walter Chalmers Smith, "Immortal, Invisible, God Only Wise," in *The Hymnal for Worship and Celebration* (Waco, Tex.: Word Music, 1986), 25.
3. A. W. Tozer, *The Knowledge of the Holy* (New York: Harper & Brothers, 1961), 18.
4. Francis A. Schaeffer, *He Is There And He Is Not Silent* (Wheaton, Ill.: Tyndale House Publishers, 1972).
5. See note 2 above.
6. Matthew Henry, *Commentary on the Whole Bible* (Grand Rapids, Mich.: Zondervan Publishing House, 1960), 505.
7. Mary A. Thomson, "O Zion, Haste," in *The Hymnal for Worship and Celebration* (Waco, TX.: Word Music, 1986), 298.

8. See note 2 above.

9. James Hastings, *The Greater Men and Women of the Bible: Hezekiah-Malachi* (Edinburgh: T & T. Clark, 1915), 64.

10. William Cosper, "Light Shining out of Darkness," *Baker's Pocket Treasury of Religious Verse*, comp. Donald T. Kauffman (1952; reprint, Grand Rapids, Mich.: Baker Book House, 1980), 185–186

CHAPTER 2

11. F. B. Meyer, *David: Shepherd, Psalmist, King* (Fort Washington, Pa.: Christian Literature Crusade, 1977), 12–13.

12. Alexander Whyte, *Bible Characters, vol. 1, The Old Testament* (Grand Rapids, Mich.: Zondervan Publishing House, 1952), 419–420.

13. Ibid., 420.

14. "Kings of the Earth" from *Saviour,* a modern oratorio. Words and music by Grey Nelson and Bob Farrell (Dallas: Word Music in conjunction with Warren Alliance, 1995).

15. John Bartlett, *Familiar Quotations*, ed. Emily Morison Beck (Boston: Little, Brown and Co., 1980), 270.

16. Joyce G. Baldwin, *Esther: An Introduction and Commentary* (Downers Grove, Ill.: Inter-Varsity Press, 1984), 63.

17. C. F. Keil, *Commentary on the Old Testament in Ten Volumes, vol. III* (Grand Rapids, Mich.: William B. Eerdmans Publishing Company, 1966), 334.

CHAPTER 3

18. Abraham Lincoln, in *Topical Encyclopedia of Living Quotations* (Minneapolis, Minn.: Bethany House Publishers, 1982), 160.

19. Hastings, *Men and Women of the Bible*, 55–56.

20. Carolina Cooperator, in *Quote Unquote*, comp. Lloyd Cory (Wheaton, Ill.: Scripture Press Publications, Inc., Victor Books, 1977), 364.

21. Anne Morrow Lindbergh, *Gift from the Sea* (New York: Random House, Pantheon Publisher, 1955), 23–24.

CHAPTER 4

22.   Bartlett, *Familiar Quotations*, 320.

23.   John F. Walvoord and Roy B. Zuck, eds. *The Bible Knowledge Commentary* (Wheaton, Ill.: 1988), 704–705.

24.   Stedman, *The Queen and I*, 35–36.

25.   Walter F. Adeney, *The Expositor's Bible Commentary: Ezra, Nehemiah and Esther*, ed. W. Robertson Nicoll. (New York: Hodder & Stoughton, n.d.), 371–372.

26.   Robert Lowry, "Nothing but the Blood," in *The Hymnal for Worship and Celebration* (Waco, Tx.: Word Music, 1986), 195.

27.   Bartlett, *op cit.*

CHAPTER 5

28.   Edward Everett Hale, cited in Bartlett, 590.

29.   "One Vote," a "Message for Americans," from John Salisbury, KXL, Portland, Oregon, April 1978. Compliments of Marlene H. Johnsen, Multnomah County Republican Central Committee.

30.   Hastings, *Men and Women of the Bible*, 57.

31.   Eugene H. Peterson, *Five Smooth Stones for Pastoral Work* (Atlanta: John Knox Press, 1980), 172–173.

32.   Isaac Watts, "Am I A Solder of the Cross?" in *The Hymnal of Worship and Celebration* (Waco, Tx.: Word Music, 1986), 482.

33.   Harry Emerson Fosdick, "God of Grace and God of Glory" in *The Hymnal for Worship and Celebration* (Waco, Tex.: Word Music, 1986), 292.

34.   Hastings, *Men and Women of the Bible*, 59.

35.   Harry Emerson Fosdick, *op cit.*

CHAPTER 6

36.   Rudyard Kipling, "If," in *The Best Loved Poems of the American People*, selected by Hazel Felleman. (Garden City, N.Y.: Garden City Books, 1936), 65.

37. Used by permission.

38. Ben Patterson, *Waiting, Finding Hope When God Seems Silent* (Downers Grove, Ill.: InterVarsity Press, 1989), 141.

CHAPTER 7

39. Baldwin, *Esther*, 90.

40. Alexander Raleigh, *The Book of Esther* (Edinburgh: Adam and Charles Black, 1880), 155–156.

41. Hester H. Cholmondeley, "Betrayal," in *Baker's Pocket Treasury of Religious Verse*, comp. Donald T. Kauffman 1962 reprint (Grand Rapids, Mich.: Baker Book House, 1980), 136.

42. Paul Lee Tan, *Encyclopedia of 7,700 Illustrations: Signs of the Times* (Chicago: Assurance Publishers, 1990), 1516, art. 6883, adapted.

CHAPTER 8

43. Diane Ball, "In His Time," in *The Hymnal for Worship and Celebration* (Waco, Tx.: Word Music, 1986), 465.

44. Philip Yancey, *Disappointment with God: Three Questions No One Asks Aloud* (Grand Rapids, Mich.: Zondervan Publishing House, 1988), 200–201.

45. Philip Yancey, *Where Is God When It Hurts* (Grand Rapids, Mich.: Zondervan Publishing House, 1977), 92.

46. Keil, *Commentary on the Old Testament*, 363.

47. Baldwin, *Esther*, 93.

CHAPTER 9

48. Corrie ten Boom, *The Hiding Place* (1971; reprint, New York: Bantam Books, Inc., 1974), 217.

49. Walvoord and Zuck, *Bible Knowledge Commentary*, 712.

50. A. W. Tozer, *The Root of the Righteous*, (Camp Hill, Pa.: Christian Publications, 1986), 137.

51.   Stedman, *The Queen and I*, 92.

CHAPTER 10

52.   Rick Telander, *The Hundred Yard Lie* (New York: Simon & Schuster, 1989), 17.
53.   Richard P. Walters, *Counseling for Problems of Self-Control*, ed. Gary R. Collins (Waco, Tx.: Word Books, 1987), 17.
54.   Ernest R. Campbell, *Galatians* (Silverton, Or.e.:Canyonview Press, 1981), 157.
55.   Baldwin, *Esther*, 102.

CHAPTER 11

56.   Luci Swindoll, *You Bring the Confetti* (Waco, Tex.: Word Books, 1986), 13.
57.   Keil, *Commentary on the Old Testament*, 345.
58.   Vance Havner, *It Is Toward Evening* (Westwood, N.J.: Fleming H. Revell Company, 1968), 39–40.

CHAPTER 12

59.   Adapted from an illustration by Dr. Robert R. Kopp, Pastor, Center Presbyterian Church, McMurray, Pa. Used by Permission.
60.   Austin Farrer, in *Quote Unquote*, comp. Lloyd Cory (Wheaton, Ill.: Scripture Press Publications, Inc., Victor Books, 1977), 150.

The Great Lives Series

In his Great Lives from God's Word Series, Charles Swindoll shows us how the great heroes of the faith offer a model of courage, hope, and triumph in the face of adversity.

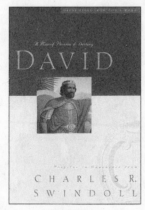

DAVID
A Man of
Passion and
Destiny

ESTHER
A Woman of
Strength and
Dignity

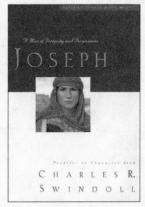

JOSEPH
A Man of
Integrity and
Forgiveness

MOSES
A Man of
Selfless Dedication

ELIJAH
A Man Who
Stood With God

PAUL
A Man of
Grace and Grit

W PUBLISHING GROUP™
www.wpublishinggroup.com